The Stock Market

A guide for the private investor

The Stock Market

A guide for the private investor

Third edition

Neil F. Stapley

Woodhead-Faulkner
in association with Laing & Cruickshank
Investment Management Services Ltd

Published by Woodhead-Faulkner Ltd
Fitzwilliam House, 32 Trumpington Street, Cambridge CB2 1QY, England
and 27 South Main Street, Wolfeboro, New Hampshire, 03894–2069, USA

Published in association with
Laing & Cruickshank Investment Management Services Ltd
Piercy House, Copthall Avenue, London EC2R 7BE, England

First published 1981
Second edition 1984
Third edition 1986
Second impression 1986

© Laing & Cruickshank Investment Management Services Ltd 1986

British Library Cataloguing in Publication Data
Stapley, Neil F.
  The stock market: a guide for the private
  investor.—3rd ed.
  1. Stock exchange—Great Britain
  I. Title
  332.64′241   HG5432

  ISBN 0-85941-347-0

Library of Congress Cataloging in Publication Data
Stapley, N. F. (Neil F.)
  The stock market.

  Includes index.
  1. Stock Exchange (London, England)   2. Investments—
Great Britain—Handbooks, manuals, etc.   I. Title.
HG4577.S73 1986   332.64′24212   86-9125
ISBN 0-85941-347-0 (pbk.)

Cover photograph courtesy of Barclays de Zoete Wedd Ltd

Design by Geoff Green
Typesetting by Hands Fotoset, Leicester
Printed and bound in Great Britain by
Biddles Ltd, Guildford and King's Lynn

Contents

Preface

In the first edition of this guide, published in 1979, I posed the question as to whether the 1980s would be noted as a period when the long-term decline in the number of private Stock Exchange investors, then in evidence, would finally be halted and even reversed. Seven years on I am delighted to say that at this point in the decade at least, the answer to my question looks like being an emphatic 'yes!'. Certainly, interest in The Stock Exchange has never been greater, of that there can be little doubt.

Hardly anyone with even a passing, let alone, practising, interest in investment or financial matters will be unaware that The Stock Exchange is currently undergoing sweeping constitutional reforms which are reshaping the whole of the UK securities industry. Such is the radical nature of these reforms, due to come into effect on 27th October 1986 (shortly after this guide is going to print), that the event has become widely known throughout the industry as the 'Big Bang'. Their effect on the private investor should not be under estimated; but of perhaps equivalent significance from a consumer's point of view is the Financial Services Bill, due to be enacted in 1987, which lays down wide-ranging new conduct of business rules for all investment businesses and the markets in which they operate.

Alone, these constitutional and regulatory changes may not have stimulated so much interest if two other events were not occurring at the same time. In the first place, with world economies on a sounder footing than existed for much of the

1970s, all the major international stock markets, including London, have pushed ahead to reach all time 'highs' in 1986. This is not to suggest that this trend will continue indefinitely and investors should at no time believe that it will (it won't!). However, politics aside, the evidence today suggests that we are in a more stable era and that the roller-coaster like behaviour of the stock market in the 1970s will remain a matter for the history books.

Secondly, there has been a huge and welcome effort by the Government and the securities industry alike to encourage wider share ownership, at the heart of which is the privatisation of State owned businesses such as British Telecom, which has successfully introduced for the first time many hundreds of thousands of people to the stock market. Beyond this, investment is being encouraged through employee share option schemes, through a less punitive tax regime and, from 1987, through the new Personal Equity Plan.

All these developments are to be welcomed because a healthy turnover in the private sector is essential if the truly competitive stock market that exists today is to be maintained in the future. Quite sensibly, however, many potential investors are reluctant to commit themselves without understanding exactly where, or into what, they are putting their money, while there is evidence to suggest that a good many others make their own investment decisions without having investigated adequately the implications of what they are doing or the alternatives open to them.

Hopefully, this guide will give investors the insight necessary to achieve that understanding. It is designed to be of interest and help to both new and existing investors and to those people whose profession brings them into regular or occasional contact with investors or stockbrokers, such as bankers, accountants and solicitors. The contents have been arranged in sections and sub-sections so that each topic can be referred to in a wide or individual context with, as far as possible, a degree of continuity throughout.

The Stock Exchange is not the casino it is sometimes made out to be and it is not just for 'the very rich'. It, and all the media which pivot around it, offer the private investor an enormous variety of choice. In a nutshell, my advice is this: don't take it on entirely alone, especially if you are a new or inexperienced investor; seek professional guidance and be prepared to approach it on a sensible, flexible and economic basis.

This guide will not make you that elusive instant fortune, but it should make you more *aware* and hence a more *efficient* investor. Combine this with the little piece of advice offered in the preceding paragraph and you should find that you end up with an investment programme, or *portfolio*, 'tailor made' for *you*.

Neil F. Stapley
The Stock Exchange, London

Section 1
The Stock Exchange, London

1.1 What is The Stock Exchange?

In a free economy, any market, in any commodity, be it vegetables, antiques or houses, must offer a choice and the prices within the market are determined ultimately by supply and demand. So it is with The Stock Exchange. It is simply a highly sophisticated market place where the traded commodity is stocks and shares. The same principles of supply and demand apply, which in turn lead to movements in prices. Thus, when demand appears to be outstripping the sources of supply (i.e. there are more buyers than sellers) prices will rise and vice versa. This is why the stock market is said to be the barometer of the economy; anticipation of a healthy, expanding economy will attract investors wishing to participate in this growth, while a depressed outlook for industry will bring about a corresponding fall in confidence – and Stock Exchange prices.

However, before a market can exist, the commodity traded has to be created or produced. In exactly the same way stocks and shares must be issued before trading can take place, which brings us to the primary function of The Stock Exchange: it provides a convenient, centralised source for raising capital for the Government, public authorities and industry. However, once an initial issue has taken place and the money required has been raised, the issuing body in no way receives any direct financial benefit from any subsequent dealings between buyers and sellers of those stocks or shares in the stock market.

So, to summarise, The Stock Exchange plays two vital, inter-linked, roles within our economic structure:

i   it enables Government and industry to raise capital with comparative ease and

ii   it provides a secondary market where existing investors can sell and prospective investors can buy.

The year 1986 witnessed the most significant and far reaching changes to The Stock Exchange's constitution since it achieved 'official' recognition and produced its first rule book in 1812. Indeed, these changes had knock-on effects far beyond The Stock Exchange itself. They were to reshape the whole UK securities industry and, because of their radical – some might say explosive – nature, their implementation became widely known as the 'Big Bang'.

What, then, were these changes and what is their significance for the future, particularly from the point of view of a private investor? To appreciate this fully, it is necessary firstly to understand a little of the structure of the 'old' Stock Exchange.

1.2   The Stock Exchange – pre 'Big Bang'

Ever since its emergence as a key component of our economic structure, The Stock Exchange was financed almost exclusively by private capital. Its membership comprised only individuals who collectively owned The Stock Exchange and administered it through an elected Council of members. The members were bound by rules and regulations which evolved over the many years of the Exchange's existence while, in addition, there was an unwritten code of conduct which all members recognised and which was reflected in the motto of The Stock Exchange: *'Dictum meum pactum'* – 'My word is my bond'. This may sound like romantic tradition, but it was the very basis on which the market developed and in many respects on which it still operated in 1986. The Exchange's individual members were all attached to member firms, mostly as partnerships, trading as either stockbrokers or stockjobbers, i.e. in a single capacity as one or the other. In 1986 there were about 200 firms of stockbrokers and 17 firms of stockjobbers.

Stockbrokers ('brokers' for short) acted only on behalf of the investing public, including the big financial institutions, buying or selling shares through stockjobbers ('jobbers') in accordance with their clients' instructions. Most broking firms combined institutional business with a private clients department and, within the latter, a range of services was usually made available (see section 2.3).

Brokers were paid for their services by a commission levied on the value of each transaction. This commission varied with the type of security traded but was based on a scale of minimum commissions laid down by The Stock Exchange itself. Brokers could not charge their clients less than these scale rates. They could charge more, but in practice the forces of competition determined otherwise.

Jobbers, on the other hand, were not permitted to trade directly with investors, only with brokers. It was often said that brokers were the 'retailers' of the stock market and jobbers the 'wholesalers'. Jobbers, then, acted purely on their own account, providing a ready market for the stocks or shares in which they *made a book*. Their revenue came from the *jobber's turn* – the difference between the prices at which they were prepared to buy or sell shares from or to brokers – and by taking positions on their books, either by *going long* (accumulating shares which they hoped to sell on at higher prices) or by *going short* (selling shares they had not got in the hope of buying them later at a lower price).

There was much to commend this separation of functions, especially from the investor's point of view. Indeed, the traditionalists will be questioning for a long time to come the need to change a system that withstood the test of a very long time. However, in recent years two very different events occurred which together signalled, clearly, that changes were inevitable.

First, the rapid advances in communications technology presaged an equally rapid internationalisation of securities markets. With London – still managing to maintain its position as the world's primary financial centre – sitting in a strategically important time zone between New York and Tokyo, it clearly had a vital role to play in the developing race towards round-the-clock securities trading, although a steadily growing amount of business in both international and leading UK shares was beginning to drift away from The Stock Exchange and into the hands of other, mostly foreign owned, securities trading organisations.

However, it quickly became apparent that even the biggest and wealthiest of Stock Exchange member firms could not possibly amass privately the huge sums of money needed to seriously compete with the much larger American and Japanese securities trading houses. So there was for some years an emerging view amongst Stock Exchange members that what they needed was the injection of the sort of financial might that only the biggest UK institutions – primarily the banks – could offer, but they in turn could not be expected to provide this without a considerable, if not complete, slice of the action. The problem was that The Stock Exchange did not allow 'outside' institutions to own its member firms, although latterly the rules were relaxed somewhat and they were able to take up to a 29.9% interest.

While all this was fermenting in the background, there was another, much more direct, assault on The Stock Exchange which, in the event, was to bring matters to a head and prove the catalyst to the changes referred to earlier.

In 1983, following criticism of The Stock Exchange's fixed commission structure by the Office of Fair Trading, the Government threatened to refer its whole rule book to the Monopolies Commission on the basis that it constituted a restrictive practice. The resulting enquiry would have been both long and expensive for The Stock Exchange and many members took the view that it was not worth defending principles that in the end were unlikely to be upheld. Moreover, the uncertainty of a protracted enquiry would have further undermined the ability of the Exchange and its members to compete in the international arena with the backing and immediacy the situation demanded.

The outcome was that in July 1983 the Government agreed to drop the case against The Stock Exchange in return for the Exchange's undertaking that it would abandon its fixed commission structure. This paved the way for sweeping reforms since it was obvious that in the new world of negotiated commissions and international competition, the traditionally separate broking and jobbing functions could not be sustained.

So, large parts of The Stock Exchange rule book were re-written to provide, inter alia, that member firms may (i) charge clients what they wish for their services and (ii) act in a dual capacity, i.e. in effect as both broker and jobber. The implementation date was set at 27th October 1986.

Moreover, six months earlier the rules covering membership itself were amended to accommodate 'outside' corporate entities. Anticipation of this event had, in the previous two years, prompted a surge of activity amongst member firms with most of the larger firms – brokers and jobbers alike – and many smaller ones forging links with banks and other financial institutions, including significantly a number of American and Continental institutions.

1.3 The Stock Exchange – post 'Big Bang'

Section 1.2 looked at the structure of The Stock Exchange before, and the events which precipitated, 'Big Bang'. It identified three key changes – the replacement of the Exchange's fixed commission scales with negotiable rates, the ability of member firms to trade in a 'dual' capacity and the admission of 'external' corporate bodies to membership of the Exchange. Yet, even these, radical as they were, do not paint the full picture of the 'securities industry revolution', since in support of the new market structure and its practices, two further developments were occurring concurrently. First, a completely new dealing system had to be designed and put in place in time for 'Big Bang'. Second, proposals for new legislation in the form of the Financial Services Bill ('FSB'), covering not just The Stock Exchange and its members but also the entire financial services industry, is before Parliament as this guide is going to print and is expected to be enacted in the early part of 1987.

The FSB provides, inter alia, for the establishment of a new body, the Securities and Investment Board ('SIB') which in turn will have regulatory powers, through its own Conduct of Business rules, over virtually all domestic (UK) investment markets and businesses. Within this framework there will be Recognised Investment Exchanges ('RIEs') and certain organisations will become Self Regulatory Organisations ('SROs') to which the SIB will delegate regulation, provided the SRO's own rules match or better those laid down by the SIB. Investment businesses which do not fall within an SRO will be authorised (or otherwise) directly by the SIB.

The Stock Exchange will be a RIE and, with its long and admired history of successful self-regulation, will become an SRO. Indeed, certain of the new rules which it introduced on 27th October 1986 reflected some of the key proposals within the SIB's Conduct of Business rules.

However, the FSB proposals also meant that the other big securities trading houses operating in the United Kingdom needed to address the issue of regulation and consider the establishment of a separate RIE. As a result, the International

Securities Regulatory Organisation ('ISRO') was formed in 1985. This represents over 180 member organisations of which just 38 are UK based. The prospect emerged, therefore, that London might have two RIEs effectively in competition with their own SROs and, to complicate matters further, some organisations as members of both.

This was not an appealing proposition for either The Stock Exchange or ISRO and following discussions between the two it was announced on 16th September 1986, just before this guide went to print, that they had agreed in principle to join forces to create a single RIE and a single SRO. The RIE will have the official title of the International Stock Exchange of the United Kingdom and the Republic of Ireland, but will be known as The Stock Exchange. The SRO will be called the Securities Association. The administrative and regulatory bodies will include representatives of both organisations.

The merger will require further changes to the present Stock Exchange's constitution and is subject to the approval of members of both organisations. It is expected to take two years to implement but, quite clearly, it represents another major development in the reshaping of the UK securities industry.

Returning now to the immediate post 'Big Bang' structure, a Stock Exchange member firm is now known generally as a *broker-dealer*. It can trade as a traditional broker, i.e. in an 'agency' capacity, whereby its clients' buying or selling orders are transacted with another member firm (generally a *market maker* as described below), or as a 'principal', buying and selling on its own account. It can satisfy its clients' orders from its own 'book', subject to tightly defined rules and only if it has firstly obtained the client's consent to this.

In addition, firms can apply to become approved market makers in nominated securities, this function equating to that of a jobber as described in section 1.2. Market makers are required, inter alia, to be prepared to trade and quote firm prices at all times in the securities in which they are registered market makers, in order to preserve the liquidity and competitive environment previously provided by the jobbing system.

The emergence of this dual capacity structure and the removal of fixed commission scales has also changed the basis on which member firms may charge for their services. However, for private client business, most firms will continue to act in an agency capacity, charging a separate commission as before. The rate of commission will vary depending upon the type of security traded, the value of the transaction and the nature of the service being offered by the firm. For example, a dealing only (sometimes referred to as 'execution only') service, whereby the client makes his own investment decisions, will be less expensive than one where the client requires advice or takes other services such as regular investment portfolio valuations. However, a firm may also deal for its clients on a 'net price' basis, whereby its charges are included in the price, provided it discloses full details of the charges to the client.

The implication of negotiable commissions is that, unlike before, rates will vary from firm to firm and even within a single firm, the latter reflecting the different levels of service and the status of the client. This guide is going to print before any clear indication has emerged of what typical commission rates amongst brokers might be after 27th October 1986, but investors will certainly have the opportunity to 'shop around' much more than before.

The arrival of corporate conglomerates, or 'fully integrated financial services groups', as members of The Stock Exchange is expected to add further dimensions to the services private investors have become accustomed to. The obvious examples are the several big banks which have acquired either brokers or jobbers, or both. These will be operating in both agency and market-making capacities and are thought to be developing all-embracing 'retail' financial services to be offered through their High Street branch networks.

However, there is another side to all this and it is termed 'conflict of interest'. The conflict, or potential for it, lies within a financial group which may be acting as both an agency broker and market maker, dealing in the shares of a company which might be followed closely by its independent research department and to which the group is also a corporate adviser or even banker. Any one of these capacities could generate share sensitive information and there is quite obviously a need to prevent this being 'leaked' to the other functions. Hence the emergence of the concept of 'chinese walls' in the SIB's proposed Conduct of Business rules, which seek to address this difficult issue, transgression of which will carry severe penalties (not least of which will be the damage to the transgressor's reputation and hence client base).

All in all, however, 'Big Bang' looks as though it will prove to have been a positive milestone for private investors, certainly as far as choice is concerned. That said, the enactment in 1987 of the Financial Services Bill promises to be an equally significant and more 'visible' event, from the perspective of the industry's private client base.

1.4 The Stock Exchange dealing system and procedures

Under the 'old' Stock Exchange dealing procedure a broker carried out a client's instruction to buy or sell a security, known as an *order*, by checking the price 'verbally' with several jobbers and then striking, or 'executing' a firm deal with whichever jobber quoted the most advantageous price (known as the *best price*) for the client. This required the broker or his dealer to walk around the trading floor, calling at the appropriate jobbers' *pitches* (those peculiar hexagonal structures arranged across the floor) and noting each quotation before actually dealing. Once the deal was struck the order became known as a *bargain* and was reported to The Stock Exchange later in the day, a procedure termed *marking*. These *marks* were then recorded, along with an 'official' closing quotation for the security, in The Stock Exchange Daily Official List ('SEDOL'), which was and still is the only authoritative published record of Stock Exchange prices.

While the same principle of checking the market to achieve best execution for the client and much of the terminology still applies, the dealing system itself was overhauled to coincide with 'Big Bang' and is now much more automated. Behind the new system is something called The Stock Exchange Automated Quotations System, or 'SEAQ' for short, which itself was developed as an extension of 'TOPIC', the Exchange's existing screen based price and information service.

Users of SEAQ can see, on a single screen, a complete list of all market makers in a particular security, the buying and selling prices they are quoting and the size, or volume, of shares to which their price relates. Importantly, too, it monitors and stores details of all trading that takes place so that any subsequent queries can be investigated fully, with irrefutable evidence at hand.

However, given the enormous range of securities quoted on The Stock Exchange and the differing frequency of trading in many of them, different classifications have been established for

SEAQ's purposes. The criteria used for equities (ordinary shares) are volume of turnover, market capitalisation (see page 53) and the number of market makers.

The main category is designated alpha securities. This will comprise leading equities and, for the record, since it seems a small number, the initial 62 constituent shares listed on page 24, account for about half of all trading in Stock Exchange listed equities in terms of volume and for a little over half of the total UK equity market capitalisation. There will be an average of 16 market makers in each one (considerably more than under the old jobbing system). The list of alpha securities will be extended in due course.

Beneath the alpha category are three further classifications – beta, gamma and delta. There are about 500 'fairly active' beta stocks and substantially more 'inactive' gamma stocks, while the delta category comprises securities not quoted on SEAQ.

Between the hours of 9.00 a.m. and 3.30 p.m. (known as the *mandatory quote period*), which is also the time that the trading floor is open, market makers are required to display firm two-way prices in not less than a marketable quantity of shares, this being generally set at 1,000 shares, for both alpha and beta securities and indicative (i.e. potentially subject to further refinement) prices in gamma securities. It is the market maker's option to continue to display prices outside the mandatory quote period, but a market maker that does is committed to deal. Trading does, in fact, continue long after 3.30 p.m. but most transactions after that time are termed *early bargains* and treated as the following day's business, the exception being securities traded for cash settlement, e.g. British Government stocks.

Once the deal has been struck it must be reported to The Stock Exchange within five minutes except for transactions after 5.00 p.m. which are reported the following morning. In the case of alpha securities, details (price, size and time) are displayed on SEAQ immediately. Prices at which deals take place in other securities are published in the following day's SEDOL.

The most significant point about SEAQ is that all market makers' prices are available on a single screen which can be accessed by users – generally other member firms – anywhere in the UK, or overseas for that matter. In theory, this means that trading can take place just as effectively by telephone as on the trading floor and many observers predict that when SEAQ is fully operational the floor will become redundant. Against this,

Leading alpha securities

Security	Share type and value
Allied-Lyons	Ord 25p
ASDA-MFI Group	Ord 25P
BAT Industries	Ord 25P
Barclays	Ord Stk £1
Bass	Ord 25P
Beecham Group	Ord 25P
Blue Circle Industries	Ord £1
BOC Group	Ord 25P
Boots Co.	Ord 25P
British Aerospace	Ord 50P
British Petroleum Co.	Ord 25P
British Telecommunications	Ord 25P
Britoil	Ord 10P
BTR	Ord 25P
Burton Group	Ord 50P
Cable & Wireless	Ord 50P
Cadbury Schweppes	Ord 25P
Commercial Union Assurance Co.	Ord 25P
Consolidated Gold Fields	Ord 25P (Regd)
Courtaulds	Ord 25P
Dixons Group	Ord 10P
Fisons	Ord 25P
General Acc. Fire & Life Assurance Corp.	Ord 25P

Security	Share type and value
General Electric Co.	Ord 5P
Glaxo Holdings	Ord 50P
Grand Metropolitan	Ord 50P
Great Universal Stores	'A' (Non.V) Ord Stk 25P
Guardian Royal Exchange	Ord 25P
GKN	Ord £1
Guinness	Ord Stk 25P
Hanson Trust	Ord 25P
Hawker Siddeley Group	Ord 25P
Imperial Chemical Industries	Ord Stk £1
Jaguar	Ord 25P
Ladbroke Group	Ord 10P
Land Securities	Ord £1
Legal & General Group	Ord 25P
Lloyds Bank	£1
Lonrho	Ord 25P
Marks & Spencer	Ord 25P
Midland Bank	£1
National Westminster Bank	Ord £1
Peninsular & Orient Steam Nav. Co.	Dfd Stk £1
Plessey Co.	Ord 25P
Prudential Corp.	25P

Security	Share type and value
Racal Electronics	Ord 25P
Reckitt & Colman	Ord 25P
Reuters Holdings	'B' Ord (Lim.V) 10P
Rio Tinto-Zinc Corp.	Ord 25P (Regd) 25P
Royal Insurance	Ord 25P
Sainsbury (J)	Ord 25P
Sears	Ord 10P
Sedgwick Group	
Shell Transport & Trading Co.	Ord 25P
(Regd) STC	Ord 25P
Sun Alliance & London Insurance	25P
Tesco	Ord 5P
THORN EMI	Ord 25P
Trafalgar House	Ord 20P
Trusthouse Forte	Ord 25P
Unilever	Ord 25P
United Biscuits (Holdings)	Ord 25P

there is a limit to the amount of traffic that even the most up-to-date telephone systems can handle – and to the patience of busy dealers repeatedly getting the engaged signal – and for the time being at least a high proportion of a day's trading is likely to remain on the floor, based on SEAQ prices of course. In other words, many market makers operate from both their own dealing rooms away from the trading floor and from the floor itself.

A further development of SEAQ is due to be introduced by The Stock Exchange in 1987. This will be known as the SEAQ Automatic Execution Facility ('SAEF' – pronounced 'safe'), which should be of particular benefit and interest to private investors since it is hoped it will help reduce member firms' dealing costs and hence the cost to their clients. Starting with a limited selection of shares, SAEF will route electronically small share transactions from a broker-dealer to whichever market maker is quoting the best price in a particular share. Where, as will normally be the case, more than one market maker is quoting the best price, the orders will be routed to each in rotation. Government stocks ('gilts') and other fixed-interest securities are traded in a slightly different way, the prices displayed on SEAQ by market makers being indicative prices only. The dealing procedure resembles more closely the 'old' style market with broker-dealers contacting market makers, either inter-office or on the trading floor, to ascertain the best price available before striking a firm deal.

1.5 Stock Exchange prices

Quotations for *all* securities dealt in on The Stock Exchange are comprised of two prices; the *bid,* or *selling,* price and the *offer,* or *buying,* price. For example, a quotation of 88p–90p would mean that the security in question could be sold for 88p or purchased for 90p.

The *middle* price is halfway between the two, which in the above example would be 89p. If just one price is given, as in the financial press or as a basis for investment valuations, it is assumed to be the middle price unless otherwise indicated.

Gilt-edged and many other UK fixed-interest securities are quoted in pounds per £100 nominal of stock. Ordinary shares, preference shares and a very few industrial loan stocks are quoted on a pence or pounds per share or unit basis, as in the above example.

1.6 Stock Exchange dealing costs

In addition to the broker's commission charges there are certain other costs involved in Stock Exchange transactions. These are summarised below and will appear as separate items on the contract note.

Government stamp duty

Purchases of virtually all UK securities now attract a ½% stamp duty. The main exceptions exempt from stamp duty are British Government stocks and Eurobonds.

PTM (Panel for Takeovers and Mergers)

All bargains with a consideration in excess of £5,000 attract a levy of 60p. Exceptions are unit trusts, offshore and overseas funds, and insurance and property bonds.

Value added tax

Residents of the United Kingdom are liable to basic-rate VAT on the commission charge, as are residents of other EEC countries on purchases only.

1.7 Settlement of clients' accounts

After an instruction to buy or sell has been carried out, the broker will issue the client with a contract note which, incidentally, should be retained by the client for record purposes. This will show full details of the transaction including the time the deal was struck, the costs involved and, of course, the net proceeds (sale) or net cost (purchase). The broker will, in due course, register purchases with the company or other body concerned and a few weeks later will send on the certificate of ownership to the client. This should be kept in a secure place – most investors deposit their certificates in safe custody at their bank. In the case of sales, the client must sign a form of transfer (usually sent out by the broker with the contract note) which is then despatched with the covering certificate to the company so that the seller's name can be removed from the register of holders of that security.

The actual monetary settlement of clients' accounts is made in two ways:

i *For cash (immediate) settlement*
   This includes all securities traded in the 'gilt-edged' market, i.e. British Government, corporation, local authority, public board, Commonwealth and Irish Government securities; new issues while in renounceable document form; most unit trusts and some foreign securities (for delivery abroad).

   It should be noted that delayed settlement for gilt-edged securities can usually be arranged if necessary. This is, for example, a relevant consideration if switching into a gilt-edged security from investments, such as registered ordinary shares, which are for 'account' settlement.

ii *For account settlement*
   This covers all normal dealings in other securities including registered ordinary shares and industrial fixed-interest securities. Each account period is of two (occasionally three) weeks' duration, commencing on a Monday and closing on the Friday ten (occasionally 15) dealing days later. Settlement takes place six dealing days later on the second Monday after the close of the account, e.g.

First day of dealing	Last day of dealing	Account or settlement day
Monday 2nd Oct.	Friday 13th Oct.	Monday 23rd Oct.

   Some adjustment to this procedure may be made when the account period covers a bank holiday.

Note: If certificates and transfers in respect of sales are not in the broker's possession by midday of the business day (normally a Friday) prior to account day, settlement of the account will be delayed.

Closing bargains

Sales or repurchases following, respectively, a purchase or sale in the same Stock Exchange account are known as closing bargains and are, at the broker's discretion, free of commission charges. Contra transactions within 28 days of the original bargain in respect of British Government, local authority and other gilt-edged securities are treated similarly.

New account dealings

During the last two business days of a Stock Exchange account it is normally possible to deal for settlement as for the succeeding account. Such transactions are said to be for the *new account* or for *new time*. Purchases made in this way usually involve paying a small premium over the normal buying price for the privilege of deferred settlement.

Section 2
New investors

2.1 When to obtain a stockbroker's advice

With newspapers and the other media today full of eye-catching
advertisements by assorted financial institutions, each pro-
claiming the merits of their particular products or services, it is
perhaps not surprising that many people overlook the stock
market as a potential investment area. Others, often mis-
guidedly, either believe they 'do not have enough money', or
regard the stock market as just another form of gambling, or
simply do not know how to go about getting in touch with a
stockbroker.

So, to start at the beginning, how do you decide that it may be
time to seek a stockbroker's advice? Well, there are no
'qualifications' or 'means tests'; it all depends on your circumstances. However, if as a starting point, you can ask yourself the
question below and answer 'Yes – over £5,000', you are at least a
prospective stock market investor – but only prospective,
because there may still be reasons why the stock market is not the
home for your money. Even if the answer is 'Yes – but less than
£5,000' the stock market may still be suitable, although in such
cases it is normally advisable to restrict your choice to British
Government securities (the gilt-edged market) or unit or investment trusts, although the same strategy is often recommended
for larger sums as well. The question is this:
*'Do I have an excess of uncommitted capital over and above what I
realistically require to cover my anticipated expenditure in the*

29

course of the next 12–18 months or so, plus a sensible allowance for the unanticipated and inflation?'

'Anticipated expenditure' in this context means any firm commitment or expected outlay that will not be met from income, such as outstanding tax or other liabilities, personal borrowings due for repayment, a deposit to find for a house, home improvements and other domestic expenditure – for example on a new car, furniture and holidays – school fees, intended gifts, etc.

Of course, there are occasions when a person suddenly acquires a sizeable lump sum that needs to be invested. Some examples of people who might find themselves in this position are given below:

i   Beneficiaries under a will or trust. If stocks and shares are received rather than 'cash' it is particularly important to consult a stockbroker, since what was suitable for the deceased or the trust may not be appropriate for the beneficiary.

ii   Widows (or widowers) looking to invest the proceeds of life assurance policies, etc., or to realign their investment position to take account of their changed circumstances.

iii   Employees having reached retirement age with part of their occupational pension commuted.

iv   Employees who find themselves redundant with a substantial severance payment.

v   Employees posted abroad wishing to accumulate capital in preparation for their return to the United Kingdom.

vi   Emigrants retaining surplus funds in the United Kingdom.

vii   Parents/grandparents seeking to invest on their children's/ grandchildren's behalf.

viii   Trustees or executors with long-term responsibilities.

ix   Retired people selling their house to move, for example, into a smaller property or nursing home.

x   Owners of small or family businesses with surplus funds accumulated.

xi   Winners of a big premium bond prize or the football pools.

In any of the foregoing situations a stockbroker's advice can often be essential, the one proviso being that the question posed earlier can still be answered positively.

At this point, it is relevant to consider the reasons, referred to above, that may still rule out the stock market as an appropriate investment area, excluding the rather obvious one that market conditions may be unfavourable. Again, it comes back to individual circumstances and it is difficult to give firm guidance in this direction without considerable qualification. However, a few examples of situations where stocks and shares *may not* be recommended are as below:

i   Where other investment areas clearly meet the investor's requirements better. For example, index-linked or other National Savings Certificates, fixed-term deposits or bonds, certain insurance-linked investments (including annuities) and gold coins are just a few investments which may sometimes be seen as sound alternatives to stock market securities – indeed, some of these may be included in an investment programme put forward by a broker, i.e. used in conjunction with stocks and shares.

ii   Where a property purchase (or other major item of expenditure), potentially absorbing a high proportion of available capital, is envisaged in the near term, i.e. where a high degree of liquidity is desirable, the money may be better employed in a building society account (particularly if the purchase is to be mortgage assisted) or similar near-cash alternative.

iii   Where, for whatever reason, it is imperative, beyond all else, to *guarantee* that the realisable value of the investment does not, at any time, fall below the original capital sum. This, incidentally, rules out virtually everything with the exception of National Savings and deposit-type investments.

It should be stressed that many factors can influence the foregoing situations, not least the individual's tax position, and quite often it is the broker who, having been approached by the client, will recommend investment in one of these alternative areas.

2.2 How to contact a stockbroker

Members of the public can obtain a stockbroker's advice in one of several ways, the route used by many people being via their bank manager (all bank branches have immediate access to stockbroking firms) or solicitor or accountant. A more direct approach is to write to the Information and Press Department of The Stock Exchange in London, or to one of its regional offices (a full list will be found on page 184), requesting a list of member firms interested in taking on new clients or to respond to one or more of the increasing number of advertisements being placed in the 'City pages' of newspapers and in specialist financial magazines by member firms. Finally, if a prospective investor knows that a family member or friend is already being advised by a broker, the possibility of a personal introduction should be investigated. The important thing is to find a firm that specialises in private client business.

Where a direct approach is made, rather than through a recognised intermediary – or 'agent' – such as a bank or solicitor, the broker will normally require a banker's reference before undertaking any transactions on The Stock Exchange on a new client's behalf. Thereafter, it is a question of the broker and client agreeing on a mutually acceptable basis on which to conduct their business. If, for any reason, a broker feels he is unable to help a prospective client, he will usually say so at the outset – equally so, the client is quite at liberty to decline the broker's advice or recommendations. Although neither event is commonplace, the latter does tend to be the more frequent occurrence of the two, often because the client has not given the broker a sufficiently comprehensive picture of his or her financial circumstances or investment objectives. In practice, this tends to be more of a problem when a broker's advice is sought through one of the intermediaries mentioned above.

Some brokers ask all new clients to fill in a questionnaire in order to give them the necessary background information against which to formulate their advice, but there are nevertheless some important points for the new investor to bear in mind when approaching a broker for the first time:

i   Be certain to state your investment objectives clearly.

ii   Give the broker as much information as you can about your overall financial position, income tax liability and family circumstances, together with any other important considerations that you feel might influence his advice.

iii Make out a list of any existing investments you may have, together with full acquisition details, such as the date they were acquired and their cost.

iv   Tell the broker if there are any investment areas that you are particularly interested in, or would wish to avoid.

v   Be sure that you fully understand the nature and implications of any investments you undertake.

vi   Try to respond as early as possible to any advice that the broker gives you.

It should be noted that proposals put forward by the SIB (see section 1.3) rightly place considerable emphasis on the need for investment advisers, including brokers, to 'know their customer' before giving advice. The proposals will require all investment advisory businesses to issue a 'client agreement letter' to each client, new and existing. This will be signed by both parties and will set out, amongst much else, the nature of the service being provided, the investment objectives of the client, types of investments that may, or may not, be considered and the basis on which the adviser is to charge for the service. Stock Exchange member firms are already required to issue such a letter in respect of 'discretionary clients' and this will be extended to all advisory clients when the SIB proposals come into force in 1987.

There is, however, a further category of client, defined as an 'execution-only client', for whom brokers will not be required to hold a client agreement letter. This recognises that many private investors prefer to make their own decisions about what to buy and what to sell without at any time taking advice from a broker or other adviser – using the broker simply to carry out their dealing instructions. However, investors tempted to become execution-only clients should understand that the new rules will prohibit a broker from giving such clients investment advice of any description, even the occasional opinion on the telephone.

2.3 Stockbroker services for the private investor

Whichever of the methods of approach described in section 2.2 is employed, the probability is that the investor will be in touch with a firm of brokers which has a special department offering a range of services to meet the requirements of most private investors. These services will vary somewhat from firm to firm but will depend ultimately on the client's investment objectives and, as a reflection of these, the size and nature of the investment portfolio selected, the degree of discretion – if any – the broker is given and whether or not an active management policy is to be pursued.

However, a typical range of private client services will include the following:

i   For first-time investors, guidance and specific recom-mendations for the construction of a suitable investment portfolio.

ii   For new clients who already have money invested – in the stock market or elsewhere – an appraisal of the holdings with recommendations for redeploying the capital, if appropriate.

iii   Occasional advice, i.e. as and when required, on all matters relating to a client's investments, e.g. takeover bids, rights issues, etc.

iv   Regular portfolio valuations and reviews (usually on an annual or six-monthly basis) with recommendations for any changes considered advisable. This service will normally be restricted to portfolios over a certain size, the typical minimum being £15,000, although this figure may vary either way from firm to firm.

v   A discretionary management service – i.e. the client authorises the broker to switch investments without prior consultation – an advantage of this being that if prompt action is considered necessary no time is lost through the process of communication.

vi   A *dealing-* or *execution-only* service for clients who wish to make their own investment decisions and use the broker only to carry out their dealing instructions.

vii   Guidance on capital gains tax and its avoidance if possible (provided the broker is aware of the relevant cost information) and on other tax matters.

viii   Portfolio valuations as at specified dates for probate or other purposes. A charge will normally be made for probate valuations.

ix   Regular or occasional investment bulletins.

x   A custody service, whereby the broker holds the client's share certificates in the name of a nominee company, thus eliminating much of the paperwork and administration for the client.

Many broking firms have also extended their range of services into 'personal financial planning', providing an advisory service covering all aspects of personal finance, including tax planning, insurance, pension and property matters, as well as investment advice and management.

Prior to the 'Big Bang', a broker's advice was normally given free, the commission on the client's dealings being the broker's main source of revenue. This is likely to change, with the lower commission revenues likely to result from the switch to negotiable rates being supplemented with fees for 'add-on' services such as portfolio management or valuations. It is also important to understand that advice is given without responsibility – in other words, a broker cannot indemnify a client against a subsequent financial loss arising from advice given in good faith. This, of course, is to a large extent analogous with other professional practices. However, all brokers are bound to act in their clients' interests to the best of their ability at all times and none would put his reputation at risk – in effect risk losing clients – by acting negligently.

It is a different matter if a client loses money as a result of a member firm defaulting. In such a case, the client may claim on The Stock Exchange Compensation Fund, which is financed by members with the express purpose of indemnifying investors against such losses. Payments are not automatic, with the circumstances of each case being taken into account; however, no genuine claim has yet been refused.

Section 3

Fixed-interest securities

3.1 What is a fixed-interest security?

As the term implies, a fixed-interest security provides a pre-determined rate of interest with, usually, the guarantee of repayment, within a stated period, or on a specific date, at a predetermined price – normally par (face value). Thus, it is possible to calculate the exact return – or yield – in prospect. With the exception of preference shares, all fixed-interest securities are loans and as such the holder is a creditor of the issuing body, be it the Government or a limited company.

3.2 What influences the price of a fixed-interest security?

When issued, a fixed-interest security will generally offer a rate of interest which reflects both the market rates prevailing at that time and the status of the issuing body. Thereafter, the price will be determined by outside movements in interest rates, the proximity of the repayment date and, occasionally, by any change in the status of the issuer. So, as a general rule, if interest rates show a falling trend, the market prices of fixed-interest securities will rise to adjust the yield levels accordingly, and vice versa.

3.3 The case for fixed-interest securities

The principal attraction of fixed-interest securities lies in the relative safety, in terms of both income and capital, which they provide, when compared with equity investments, where there are no guarantees. There is an immensely wide range of stocks available, offering repayment dates to beyond the year 2000. The choice of individual stocks will depend on the investor's circumstances and whether, within these, the objective is a high immediate income, capital appreciation or a compromise between the two. Because of their defensive properties, it is normally considered advisable for private investors to have some part of their capital in fixed-interest securities and, more specifically, in British Government securities, i.e. the gilt-edged market.

3.4 Yields on fixed-interest securities

There are two yields used in the evaluation of fixed-interest securities, namely interest and redemption yields, and it should be noted that, unless otherwise stated, yields are quoted gross, as the gross figure is common to all investors, regardless of their income tax liability.

Interest yields *(or flat, running or current yields)*

Gross interest yield: This expresses the amount of gross annual income an investor receives as a percentage of the prevailing stock price; in effect the amount of gross income receivable per £100 invested. It can be calculated by the following formula:

$$\frac{\text{Interest (coupon) rate} \times 100}{\text{Stock price}} \%$$

Example 1

Interest (coupon) rate per annum %	Stock price £%	Gross interest yield £%
6	60	10.0
11½	100	11.5
13¾	110	12.5

Net interest yield: This shows the gross interest yield adjusted for a stated rate of tax, i.e. the amount of net income, after a stated rate of tax, receivable per £100 invested. It can be calculated by the following formula:

$$\text{Gross interest yield (see above)} \times \frac{(100 - \text{tax rate})}{100} \%$$

Example

Gross interest yield £%	Investor's tax rate %	Net interest yield £%
10.0	29	7.1
10.0	45	5.5
10.0	60	4.0

Redemption yields

These are perhaps the more meaningful yields, as they express, as an annualised figure, the overall return in prospect if a stock is held to redemption. They are calculated from a formula which takes into account the discounted value of the future capital gain (or loss if the market price is higher than the redemption value) plus the present value of the interest payments to be paid until redemption, assuming the interest is received semi-annually and the portions of capital gain (or loss) to redemption are notionally received semi-annually. As this suggests, it is not possible to calculate redemption yields easily. They can best be obtained from a broker who will probably have a computer capable of calculating gross and net redemption yields at the press of a key. Obviously, it is not possible to calculate redemption yields for irredeemable stocks.

Gross redemption yield: This incorporates the gross interest and gross appreciation (i.e. before all taxes). It is therefore the most salient factor when considering fixed-interest stocks for investors who have no liability to UK taxation, e.g. those with a very low income, charities, pension funds and overseas residents.

Net redemption yield: This allows for a stated rate of income tax on the interest element and, when applicable, capital gains tax on the appreciation. Net redemption yields should consequently be the basis for selecting stocks for UK taxpayers.

Grossed-up net redemption yield: In effect, this shows the compound annual rate of interest (e.g. from deposit-type investments) needed over the same period as the stock concerned has to run to redemption to equal a given net redemption yield at a stated rate of tax.

Example

Net redemption yield £%	Investor's tax rate %	Grossing-up factor	Grossed-up NRY £%
5.0	29	1.41	7.05
5.0	45	1.82	9.10
5.0	60	2.50	12.50

Grossing-up factor: This can be found simply by subtracting the investor's tax rate from 100 and dividing the answer into 100, e.g. as above

$$\frac{100}{100-29} = 1.41, \quad \frac{100}{100-45} = 1.82 \text{ and } \frac{100}{100-60} = 2.50$$

Section 4

The gilt-edged market

4.1 General comments

Strictly speaking, the gilt-edged market comprises securities issued or guaranteed by HM Government, but in practice also encompasses stocks issued by UK corporations or local authorities, other UK public authorities and sterling issues of Commonwealth Governments.

UK Government issues are by far the most important part of this and the fixed-interest market generally, in terms of status and volume. There are about 100 stocks listed with a total face value (nominal amount) in excess of £100 billion.

Stocks within this market are divided into four categories:

Short-dated: under 5 years to redemption
Medium-dated: 5–15 years to redemption
Long-dated: over 15 years to redemption
Irredeemable: no final redemption date

There are a number of factors which recommend Government stocks to private investors:
 i Security is considered the highest available in the market.
 ii The large size of the individual issues ensures a ready two-way market at any time.
 iii Dealing expenses tend to be lower than on other Stock Exchange securities.

iv Capital profits, whether arising from a sale in the market or from redemption, are free of capital gains tax.

v Dealings are normally for cash (immediate) settlement, making the capital readily realisable.

vi A stock can usually be found from the wide range available to suit most investors' requirements.

4.2 Accrued interest on gilt-edged securities

Gilt-edged securities are dealt in at an underlying price plus the interest accrued since the beginning of the current six-monthly interest period. This is calculated from the day following the last interest payment to the settlement date of a transaction. The important exception to this rule occurs in the ex-dividend period (see section 4.3) immediately prior to the interest payment date when a stock will be dealt in minus the interest in respect of the days left to go to the interest payment date. In this case the accrued interest is deducted from the consideration.

Examples

Date of transaction	Stock	Interest paid	Accrued interest
A 1st October	Treasury 10% Stock 1987	12th Jun./Dec.	+112 days = £3.068%
B 1st October	Treasury 9½% Stock 1988	25th Apr./Oct.	−23 days = £0.599%

In example A the 112 days represent the period 13th June (the day after the last interest payment) to 2nd October (the settlement date for normal gilt-edged transactions on 1st October). In example B the stock is ex dividend (without entitlement to the interest due on 25th October) and the 23 days deductible represent the period 2nd October (settlement date, as before) to, in this case, 24th October (the day prior to the next interest payment).

It should be noted that prior to 28th February 1986, when a new Accrued Income Scheme came into effect, gilt-edged securities other than short-dated stocks were dealt in at prices which *included* the interest accrued in respect of the next interest payment.

4.3 Further notes on gilt-edged securities

Ex dividend

British Government stocks are quoted ex dividend 37 days before the interest payment date. However, in the case of stocks over five years to redemption it is possible to buy or sell *special ex dividend* up to 58 days before the interest payment date. When dealing in stocks in this latter way it is very important to stipulate 'special xd'; otherwise the stock would be bought or sold cum dividend in the normal way.

National Savings Stock Register

A selection of British Government securities can be purchased on the National Savings Stock Register through a post office. Purchases cannot exceed £5,000 nominal value of any one security on any one day. Interest is paid gross, i.e. without deduction of basic rate income tax, although it is tax assessable in the normal way. A list of stocks available and other details can be obtained from a post office.

Overseas residents

There is a wide range of British Government stocks on which overseas residents are able to obtain the interest paid gross, i.e. without deduction of UK income tax at source, on application to the Bank of England via the Inspector of Foreign Dividends (Form A3). This facility makes such stocks particularly attractive to overseas residents.

4.4 Local authority yearling bonds

Local authority yearling bonds are issued weekly on Tuesdays, normally at par, and are usually repaid to the registered holder after 53 weeks, also at par. The rate of interest on each bond fluctuates in accordance with prevailing market rates at the time of issue but is normally much in line with other types of one-year local authority deposits. The bonds can be purchased or sold only in multiples of £1,000 nominal and, as with other short-dated stocks in this sector, are dealt in after issue at an underlying price plus or minus the interest accrued on a daily basis. Two interest payments are made; one after approximately six months and one on maturity. The interest is paid net of basic-rate income tax.

Section 5

Index-linked Government stocks

5.1 General comments

Index-linked Government stocks (ILGSs) provide investors with an opportunity to keep their capital in line with inflation, as measured by the General Index of Retail Prices (RPI), with a small, predetermined notional rate of interest which itself is also adjusted to reflect movements in the same index. It is by virtue of this interest-rate adjustment that holders of ILGSs are guaranteed a 'real' return (more than the rate of inflation) from their investment, which in effect, will be equivalent to that notional rate of interest. Consequently, the actual future return to redemption (interest plus capital growth) on ILGSs cannot be calculated exactly, unlike conventional redeemable stocks carrying a fixed rate of interest, which may, or may not, provide holders with a real return, depending on future inflation rates.

Since ILGSs are subject to the normal influences that determine gilt-edged yields and thereby market prices (with the added dimension of the index link), it should be clearly understood by prospective purchasers that the market prices of ILGSs will be liable to fluctuate as investors at large assess the relative attractions of these and conventional Government stocks in the light of anticipated interest-rate trends and inflationary expectations. In other words, there can be no actual guarantee (until redemption) that the market's valuation of an ILGS will reflect progressively and exactly its underlying, index-linked notional value.

5.2 Choosing between ILGSs and conventional Government stocks

In the simplest terms, the decision will rest on the expectations for inflation at any point in time. Thus, if an investor believes that the cumulative return on an ILGS (with capital and interest adjusted for inflation as above) over a given period of time will exceed the calculable return to redemption available on a conventional fixed coupon stock, then a strong case will exist for buying an ILGS – and vice versa. Of course, as much as all other investments, holdings of ILGSs will need to be reviewed from time to time to judge their suitability in prevailing market conditions. Subject to this generalisation, ILGSs will typically appeal to investors who before might have considered index-linked National Savings Certificates, i.e. those who are principally concerned to protect their capital against inflation and who, in return for this built-in protection, are prepared to accept a relatively modest immediate income level. They are less likely to appeal to investors who, for whatever reason, are seeking the maximum immediate income return from their investments, if necessary at the sacrifice of ultimate capital protection. In such cases, conventional stocks carrying a high fixed-coupon rate will probably remain the first choice.

5.3 How does the index linking work?

It all centres on an 'index ratio', recalculated and applied each time an interest payment is made during the life of the stock and then applied again to the principal sum when the stock reaches maturity. For each different stock in issue, the relevant index ratio is based on a constant divisor, which is the published RPI for the eighth month preceding the month in which the stock was issued. For example, 2% Index-linked Treasury Stock 1988 was issued in March 1982, and so its index ratio base is the published RPI for July 1981. Starting from this base, and after a pre-determined rate of interest for the first interest period, the rate of interest will be calculated by reference to subsequent movements in the RPI (always, in effect, eight months in arrears), as will the ultimate repayment value of the principal. So for all ILGSs:

an interest payment or redemption payment in the calendar month of	J F M A M J J A S O N D
will be based on the published RPI for the previous	M J J A S O N D J F M A
which, to give the relevant index ratio, will be divided by	the RPI for the eighth month preceding the month of issue of the stock

The index ratio so calculated will then be applied (i) to half the notional coupon rate of the stock to arrive at the interest rate for the next six-monthly period and (ii) at redemption to the principal sum to arrive at the repayment value. In effect, therefore, the repayment value will be known eight months before redemption, the implication of this being that during this latter period the stock will come to be regarded more as a short-dated conventional issue. The Bank of England will announce the relevant rates just before the preceding interest payment date.

Example

2% Index-linked Treasury Stock 1988. Issued March 1982. Redeemable 30th March 1988. Interest paid 30th March/30th September.

Index ratio based on RPI for July 1981 = 297.1

Interest due on	30.3.83	30.9.83
was based on RPI for	July 1982	January 1983
These RPIs were	323.0	325.9
so the index ratios were	323.0 ÷ 297.1	325.9 ÷ 297.1
	= 1.0871	= 1.0969
so the interest payable was	1% × 1.0871	1% × 1.0969
	= £1.0871%	= £1.0969%
announced by	29.9.82	29.3.83

and so on throughout the life of the stock to:

Redemption on	30.3.88
Repayment value will be based on RPI for	July 1987
If inflation averaged 8% per annum, the RPI will be around	470

and the index ratio would be	$470 \div 297.1$
	$= 1.5819$
so the repayment value per £100 nominal stock would be	100×1.5819
	$= £158.19$
announced at latest by	29.9.87

Note: At a 6% average inflation rate the repayment value would be around £142.

Section 6

Industrial fixed-interest securities

6.1 Debenture stock

This is a loan secured on the assets of a company, carrying a fixed rate of interest and normally the guarantee of redemption by a specified date. In the event of the issuing company being wound up, debenture holders rank only after the company's trade creditors for repayment as the underlying assets are sold. The rating of the stock will reflect to some extent the status of the issuing company, but first class debentures normally offer yields only slightly in excess of comparable gilt-edged securities.

6.2 Unsecured loan stock

This is similar to a debenture stock with one very important exception – as its title suggests it offers no asset security against the loan and, in the event of the company being wound up, holders rank only one place ahead of the preference and ordinary shareholders for repayment. Yields are therefore normally somewhat higher than on comparable debentures. Investors looking for capital security should be wary of second-line unsecured loan stocks; an above-average yield may signify that the issuing company is in some difficulty, or the issue is small and of narrow marketability.

6.3 Convertible loan stock

This gives the holder the right to convert the stock into the issuing company's equity capital on predetermined terms. Normally, the conversion period runs for a number of years and the decision regarding the appropriate point in time to exercise the rights should be based on a comparison of (i) the yields and (ii) the market values of the convertible stock and the equity. Of course, if it is advantageous to convert on the above criteria, the merits of holding the equity in the prevailing market conditions should also then be considered.

When issued, and in the earlier years of the conversion period, the yield on the convertible stock will normally be above that offered by the equity. Convertible stocks are, therefore, mainly of interest to the investor who requires a good, relatively safe, income with the added spice of a measure of capital growth potential provided by the underlying equity link.

Note: A similar principle applies to convertible preference shares (see below) although, by definition, the risk element is somewhat higher.

6.4 Preference shares

Although preference shares are nearly always grouped with other fixed-interest securities, they are, in fact, part of the share capital of a company and the interest is paid out of taxed, rather than pre-tax, profits. However, because preference share dividends are limited to a fixed rate, their market price performance does generally tend to reflect movements in interest rates, in much the same way as other fixed-interest securities. The dividends are usually cumulative, which means that if the company has a difficult year, and is unable to pay its preference capital dividends, the arrears must be paid out of a later year's profits before ordinary shareholders receive a dividend. In the case of non-cumulative preference shares the company has no obligation to pay any passed dividends.

Demand for preference shares comes mainly from corporate investors seeking a relatively safe, high, franked (already taxed) income and for this reason sound, easily marketable issues tend to yield no more, if not less, than rather more secure debenture and unsecured loan stocks. This apart, the major disadvantage from a private investor's point of view is that most are irredeemable, giving little or no capital protection, and also carry much of the risk of equity investment, without the potential rewards. Taking all this into account, straightforward (non-convertible) preference shares are not normally regarded as suitable investments for the private investor.

Section 7

Ordinary shares (equities)

7.1 What is an ordinary share?

An ordinary share is part of the capital of a limited company. Ownership of such a share in turn represents part ownership of that company and entitles the holder (i) to have a proportionate say in the company's affairs and (ii) to receive similarly proportionate benefits, such as dividends, from its prosperity. In other words, ownership is 'shared' with other people. It is easy to imagine that there is an unlimited supply of shares on the stock market, like a bottomless well from which brokers simply draw, or into which they discard, shares when buying or selling. This illusion merely demonstrates the sophisticated basis on which The Stock Exchange draws buyer and seller together. At any one moment there is, in fact, a strictly limited supply of shares and although this may run into many millions in the case of large companies there must always be a matching transaction, i.e. sale against purchase, purchase against sale, so that the share register of each company balances to account for the exact number of shares in issue.

7.2 What influences the price of an ordinary share?

Section 1.1 explains that ultimately it is supply and demand that governs movements in stock market prices. So it is more correct to ask, 'What influences the supply and demand for a share?' The answer is all-embracing: anything. Anything, that is, pertinent to

50

the prospects of the company in question, the industry, or industries, in which it operates and the prevailing economic and political background. These factors are constantly fluctuating and it is investor reaction to their individual or collective implications, related to existing share price levels, that produces day-by-day – indeed, transaction-by-transaction – movements in share prices. This, then, is where the supply and demand rule enters. For example, if certain shares are considered attractive at a particular price, buying demand may outstrip the supply from willing sellers (why should they sell their 'attractive' shares?). Consequently, the price will rise until more existing shareholders are tempted to sell shares and there is a more even trade between buyers and sellers. The reverse would apply if it was considered that a share was too expensive at a particular price level and sellers would predominate, forcing the price down until buyers emerged.

7.3 The case for ordinary shares

As explained in section 7.1, ordinary shares entitle investors to have a proportionate say (vote) in the company's affairs and to participate in its anticipated prosperity. However, the average private investor is unlikely to be able to build up a shareholding sufficiently large to influence or control a quoted company. Most investors therefore buy shares for the second reason, hoping that the company's profits will grow over the years, leading to higher dividends for shareholders. In turn, this increases the yield on the investment and should also result in a rise in the market value of the shares. Ordinary shares, therefore, have the potential to provide the investor with a rising income and growth of capital, both important considerations in an inflationary era.

However, while a company and its shareholders may prosper when trading conditions are favourable, in more difficult times it could suffer a set-back in profits, even to the extent of making a loss, and fail to pay a dividend to its ordinary shareholders. In extreme conditions it could cease trading and go into liquidation. Passing (not paying) the dividend would be certain to depress the share price, while liquidation could render the shares valueless. In the post-war years these occurrences, particularly the latter, have fortunately been relatively infrequent and the case for ordinary shares outweighs that against. Nevertheless, it must always be remembered that ordinary shares carry risks and not just rewards and for this reason it is normally considered advisable for private investors to combine investment in this sector with the more defensive properties of gilt-edged or similar securities, the balance between the two categories being dictated by individual circumstances.

7.4 Valuing ordinary shares

Given that supply and demand will ultimately decide a share price, there are a number of accepted criteria by which the *relative* merits of shares are judged. These illustrate the relationship of a company's share price to its net attributable profits (earnings) and dividend level or give other information of interest to the investor. This section contains brief descriptions of the principal criteria that the private investor is most likely to encounter when considering ordinary shares. See also section 8.

Dividend: The amount of net (after corporation tax) profit distributed by a company to its shareholders. The general practice now is for UK companies to declare the dividend as net pence per share, i.e. after basic-rate income tax. However, it can also be expressed in pence gross or as a net or gross percentage of the par value of the shares.

Example

Par value of shares p	Net dividend declared p		Gross dividend p		Net dividend %		Gross dividend %
25	7.1	=	10.0	=	28.0	=	40.0

Assumed basic rate of income tax = 29%

Most companies pay two dividends in respect of their financial years: an interim relating to the first six months and a final at the end of the year, which is normally the larger of the two.

Dividend cover: The number of times the total dividend for a year could have been paid out of a company's net profit for that year, if it was distributed in full to shareholders. A high cover normally suggests the dividend is safe and that there is scope for it to be increased, while a figure of less than 1.0 indicates that the company has had to call on retained profits from previous years to make up the payment. Although it depends ultimately on individual company circumstances and the nature of its business, a low cover or uncovered dividend is less desirable to the investor than one which is well covered.

Dividend yield: This expresses the gross dividend as a percentage of the prevailing share price level; in effect it is the amount of gross income receivable per £100 invested in the shares at that price.

$$\text{Dividend yield} = \frac{\text{Gross dividend (p)} \times 100}{\text{Share price}} \%$$

Example

Gross dividend p	Share price p	Dividend yield %
5.0	50	10.0
5.0	200	2.5

The following formula can be used to calculate the *average* yield on a portfolio of investments:

$$\frac{\text{Total gross annual income} \times 100}{\text{Market value of portfolio}} \%$$

Earnings per share (EPS): The amount of net (after corporation tax) profit attributable to the company expressed in per share terms, i.e. net profits divided by the number of shares in issue.

Example

Net profit	Number of shares in issue	Earnings per share
£1.8 million	6 million	30p

Market capitalisation: The market value of a company's issued ordinary shares, i.e. total number of shares in issue multiplied by the share price. The *total* market capitalisation of a company would include its preference share capital, if any, similarly valued.

Example

Number of shares in issue	Share price	Market capitalisation
25 million	300p	£75 million

Net asset value per share (NAV): The balance sheet value of a company's assets attributable to its ordinary share capital expressed in per share terms, i.e. net assets attributable to ordinary shareholders divided by the number of shares in issue.

Example

Net attributable assets	Number of shares in issue	Net assets per share
£18 million	12 million	150p

Asset backing is often an important consideration and some shares are bought purely, or largely, for their potential or actual net asset worth, as related to the prevailing share price. Some more obvious examples are property shares and investment trust shares.

Price/earnings ratio (PER): Describes the relationship between the share price of a company and its earnings per share and is found by dividing the former by the latter. In effect, therefore, it represents the number of years it would take the company to 'earn' its prevailing share price, assuming no change in the earnings figure employed in calculating the ratio, whether this is historic or prospective (see section 7.5).

Example

Share price	Earnings per share	Price/ earnings ratio
55p	5.0p	11.0

The PER is mainly used as a yardstick for comparing the share ratings of companies in the same or related industries, or against a sector or market average.

7.5 Historic and prospective criteria

When considering ordinary shares, it is important to appreciate the distinction between historic and prospective criteria. Historic figures are based on results which have actually been achieved and reported by a company. Prospective figures are based on estimated results for a stated future period. It is the latter which will most interest a potential buyer and on which existing shareholders will base their sell or hold decisions.

Example

Suppose:

i   In April 1987 a company reports net earnings per share of 30p for 1986 and pays a total dividend of 9.6p gross.

ii Analysis of the company suggests that in 1988 net earnings could rise to 40p and the dividend to 12p gross.

iii The current share price is 240p.

	Historic (1986)	Prospective (1987)
Earnings per share	30p	40p
Gross dividend	9.6p	12p
Price/earnings ratio	8.0	6.0
Dividend yield	4.0%	5.0%

7.6 Other classes of share capital

The capital structure of some companies incorporates more than one class of equity, the difference between the classes normally relating to the voting or dividend rights. These differences will be reflected in the market prices of the separate classes which, if not straightforward ordinary shares, will usually fall into one of the following categories.

'A' ordinary shares: Usually rank in all respects with ordinary shares with the exception that they carry no voting rights. For this reason, 'A' shares are normally somewhat lower in price than vote-carrying ordinary capital.

Accumulating ordinary shares: Rank in all respects with the ordinary shares but, instead of a cash dividend, holders receive a free issue of shares to the equivalent value. However, the value of such scrip issues is treated as investment income and taxed accordingly.

'B' ordinary shares: Normally as accumulating ordinary shares.

Capital shares (investment trust): See section 11.3

Deferred shares: Usually rank in all respects with the ordinary shares except that their entitlement to dividends is deferred until a predetermined future date. Thus a company's deferred shares usually will stand below the price of its dividend paying ordinary shares and, in anticipation of the price differential closing, merit consideration by investors requiring no immediate income, such as high rate tax payers.

Income shares (investment trust): See section 11.3

Non-voting ordinary shares: As 'A' ordinary shares.

Preference shares: See section 6.4

Preferred ordinary shares: Similar in most respects to preference shares but dividends are normally 'non-cumulative'.

7.7 Reverse yield gap

This is the difference between the interest yield on a representative Government stock – usually 2½% Consolidated Stock – and the (lower) average dividend yield on leading ordinary shares. This apparent anomaly – the more 'secure' investment giving the higher yield – illustrates the fact that in recent years equities have been acknowledged as offering potentially better overall protection against inflation. Before 1959 the yield gap was positive; i.e. there was a lower yield on Government stock than on equities.

Section 8
Company affairs

8.1 Company accounts

Section 7 lists the principal criteria used in the valuation of ordinary shares. However, the investor frequently will find reference to other statistics or items relating to a company's accounts or trading position in, for example, a press or broker's report. Although company accounts and analysis is a technical subject on which a number of textbooks are readily available, brief descriptions of a few commonly used terms are given below.

Annual report and accounts: Sent to all shareholders and contains the company's annual accounts together with the directors' report and often other useful information on the company and its activities, including the Chairman's statement.

Asset: Property of any description which has a monetary value and which is included in a company's balance sheet. Fixed assets are those of a permanent nature, e.g. land, buildings and machinery. Current assets are those of a cash or near-cash nature, e.g. bank balances, debtors and short-term investments.

Authorised share capital: The maximum number of shares that can be issued by a company. It can be increased only with shareholders' approval.

Balance sheet: Shows the financial position of a company by means of analysis of its assets and liabilities at its year-end. By law, the balance sheet is required to show a true and fair view of a company's affairs and it is its auditors' function, as an independent body, to ensure this is the case.

Book value: The value of an asset as stated in a company's balance sheet, normally representing original cost less depreciation, if applicable.

Cash flow: Funds for use within a company generated by its own operations – not by borrowings. It is represented by depreciation plus the residue of net profits after payment of tax and dividends.

Close company: A company which is controlled by (i) five or fewer shareholders, or (ii) its own directors.

Depreciation: The writing-down in value of a company's fixed assets, usually over a period of years, to reflect their loss of value through use within the business.

Dilution: Describes the diminishing effect that can result from an additional issue of shares by a company (i) on its voting capital structure or (ii) on its net assets or earnings if the issue price is lower than its net asset value per share or earnings per share.

Holding company: Strictly speaking, a company which has a controlling interest in another company. It is more broadly used to describe a company which has a number of subsidiaries, often wholly owned, operating in different industries.

Issued share capital: The actual number of shares issued by a company, within the limits of its authorised capital.

Liabilities: Amounts owing by a company, as disclosed in its balance sheet. Current liabilities are those which are payable within one year from the date of the balance sheet.

Loan capital: Long-term borrowings of a company. It does not include short-term borrowings such as bank overdrafts.

Minority shareholders: The owners of that part of a company's equity capital not held by a holding company or other controlling group.

Prior charges: Fixed capital or other claims on a company's assets or profits which have priority over the share capital.

Profits: A company's revenue less its expenses – usually broken down into various pre- and post-tax figures, the most salient from a shareholder's point of view being net attributable profits, which is the amount left after tax and prior charges have been paid and on which the ordinary share dividend depends.

Reserves: Amounts retained in the business, either from previous years' profits or from capital transactions:
i   *Revenue reserves* – retained profits after tax and dividend payments, which technically could be made available for future dividend payments if necessary.
ii *Capital reserves* – arise from capital transactions such as a rights issue of shares at a premium to their par value or the revaluation or sale of any fixed asset. Capital reserves are not available for dividend purposes.

Shareholders' funds: The total assets of the company less its total liabilities, including prior charges. To find the ordinary shareholders' funds, the nominal preference share capital is deducted.

Subsidiary company: A company controlled by another company, usually known as the parent or holding company. For a company to be a subsidiary, the parent company must hold more than 50% of the former's equity capital and more usually holds 100%.

Turnover: Sales before the deduction of any expenses.

8.2 Rights issues and capitalisation issues

Rights issue

A rights issue involves the allotment of extra shares or stock (not always of the same class) to existing shareholders on a pro rata basis and at a fixed price. The issue price is conventionally pitched below the market price of the shares to encourage shareholders to take up their allotments. The object of a rights issue is to raise additional capital for a normally stated purpose, but, before taking up their entitlement, shareholders should satisfy themselves that prospects for the company warrant the injection of further cash into the investment and that when the 'call' becomes payable the market price of the 'old' shares has not dropped below the issue price.

Shareholders who decide not to take up, i.e. renounce, their allotments are usually able to sell the new shares in 'nil paid' form in the period before payment is due for the *premium* which will exist all the time the market price of the existing shares remains above the issue price of the new shares. It should be noted that an alternative is simply to allow the issue to lapse, i.e. take no action at all, in which case most UK companies will sell in one large block the new shares not taken up and distribute the proceeds on a pro rata basis amongst the original allottees, subject normally to a minimum value of the rights sold of £1. This can often be a more favourable proposition than selling small allotments through the market. However, that companies should sell unallocated rights for the benefit of shareholders is not mandatory (it is rarely, if ever, a procedure adopted by overseas companies) and the position should be checked by reference to the allotment letter.

Occasionally, shareholders are given the opportunity to subscribe for *excess* shares, i.e. those not taken up by other shareholders, in which case a separate application form will accompany the standard allotment letter. The merits of making such excess applications will depend on the terms of the issue. See also 'Ex-rights', section 10.1, and 'New issues', section 9.

Capitalisation issue

Also known as a *bonus* or *scrip* or *free* issue, this is an issue of shares (not always of the same class) on a pro rata basis to existing shareholders, without charge. It occurs when a company's accumulated capital reserves have grown out of line with its issued share capital. It is effectively a balance sheet adjustment and theoretically has no effect on the market value of shareholders' investments, the share price being adjusted to take account of the additional shares in issue. In other words, the company's assets and earnings simply have to be 'divided' between more shares. However, a capitalisation issue can sometimes improve the marketability of a share, especially highly priced shares. See also 'Ex capitalisation', section 10.1.

8.3 Other share capital changes

Section 8.2 covers in detail the two types of share issues to a company's existing shareholders that will be most frequently encountered by equity investors. However, a company may sometimes find it desirable otherwise to alter the structure of its share capital which may in turn result in a change in the nominal holdings of existing shareholders, or in their voting or dividend rights. Most changes of this nature will fall into one of the following categories:

Consolidation: The 'writing-up' of the par value of a company's shares, usually as part of a restructuring scheme. For example, a 5p par value share consolidated into a 25p par value share would leave the shareholder with one-fifth of his original holding, although the share price would be adjusted accordingly.

Enfranchisement (of 'A' or non-voting shares): The conversion of non-voting share capital into voting capital. Holders of the original voting capital are often compensated for the dilution of their voting power by a capitalisation issue.

Scrip dividend: The issue of shares by way of a small capitalisation issue in lieu of, or to the equivalent value of, a cash dividend.

Stock split: The American equivalent of a capitalisation issue, although its effect on existing holdings resembles that of a sub-division (see below). For example, an American 2:1 stock split would leave the shareholder with twice as many shares as before, whereas a UK 2:1 capitalisation issue would treble the original holding (2 new shares + 1 old).

Sub-division: The division of the par value of a company's shares into smaller units, e.g. £1 par value into 25p value. The latter would give the shareholder four times as many shares, although, as with a capitalisation issue, the market price of the

25p units would fall to a quarter of the price of the £1 shares. It should be noted that companies do not normally issue new certificates when sub-dividing the capital in this way.

8.4 Gearing

When used in connection with the capital structure of a company, the term 'gearing' describes the relationship between the company's ordinary share and fixed-interest capital. High gearing suggests that a company has a high proportion of fixed-interest borrowings relative to the ordinary shares, while low borrowing and a large equity would be described as a low-geared company. In broad terms, a high gearing means that a large proportion of a company's profits is required to cover the interest payments on its borrowings but thereafter there is a comparatively small proportion of ordinary shares on which to pay dividends. A low-geared company requires only a small part of its profit to cover its prior charges but, relatively, has far more shares in issue on which to pay dividends. The result of this is that shareholders in highly-geared companies should benefit more in periods of rising profits and suffer more on profit downswings. Thus, the share prices of such companies tend to be more volatile than those of companies with a low gearing.

8.5 Takeover bids and mergers

While section 7.3 describes the fundamental case for investing in ordinary shares, added spice for many equity investors lies in the possibility that their company may one day be the subject of a takeover approach from another company. Inevitably, companies whose independence may be most at risk tend to fall into the smaller to medium-sized category; although in recent years one or two of the market's biggest companies have proved vulnerable. The company making the approach will invariably wish to gain full control of its intended new subsidiary, so that its affairs can be run without accounting to minority interests and, thus, the terms offered to shareholders of a company subject to a bid will usually be generous and often value the shares well above the levels at which dealings have been taking place on The Stock Exchange. This accounts for the sharp rise in the price of a company's shares which often accompanies the announcement of a takeover bid. Although each takeover bid or merger (the latter is usually 'agreed' by both companies) must be considered on its individual merits, there are a number of points which are usually worth keeping in mind.

i Do not be in a hurry to accept an offer – unless it is a rescue operation! Remember that a second company might also be interested and may put in a higher counterbid. Wait until a day or two before the final acceptance date before making a decision.

ii Satisfy yourself that any securities offered in exchange for your shares suitably meet your investment objectives. For example, if you hold a company's ordinary shares for capital appreciation and are offered, wholly or partly, a high-yielding fixed-interest stock in exchange, you should consider disposing of the latter and reinvesting in another growth equity.

iii Remember that accepting cash wholly or partly for your securities in a takeover bid will constitute a disposal for capital gains tax purposes, so this may need to be brought into your overall CGT strategy for the relevant tax year. Accepting securities in exchange does not constitute a disposal but the cost for capital gains tax purposes of the new holding(s) will be the cost of the original holding. This cost will have to be adjusted if more than one security is received in exchange – most tax advisers will know the appropriate cost adjustment factors (it is not sufficient to allocate the original cost on a random basis between more than one new holding).

iv In most bid situations there is little to be gained by remaining a minority shareholder if the offer has been declared unconditional; indeed, once the offeror company has received acceptances totalling over 90% of the shares bid for in the offeree company, it can by law compulsorily acquire the shares remaining in minority hands. Consequently, even if you are firmly opposed to the takeover, the best advice in this situation is to face defeat gracefully and accept the bid.

v If in doubt, approach your broker for advice on the situation.

8.6 Liquidation

Liquidation is the term given to the dissolution of a limited company. It may be initiated (i) by the shareholders or directors ('voluntary liquidation'), (ii) by its creditors (if the company has failed to meet its obligations to them) or (iii) by court order if the company is insolvent (its liabilities, excluding its equity capital, exceeding its total assets). Liquidation represents the ultimate risk for equity investors as they rank last, behind all creditors, for the distribution of the proceeds from the sale of the company's assets. It should be noted, however, that some investment companies are specifically designed to be put into voluntary liquidation on or between predetermined dates (see section 11.3).

Section 9

New issues

9.1 General comments

As outlined in section 1.1, The Stock Exchange primarily exists as a capital market and all quoted securities must have originated from a new issue of one form or another. The Government and local authorities, for example, usually invite the investor to fund their borrowing requirements by issuing stocks via a prospectus (see section 9.2 below) and application form, a copy of which is advertised in certain daily newspapers. Companies already having a Stock Exchange quotation can issue additional stocks or shares to existing shareholders or exchange them for shares in another company when acquiring, or merging with, that company; these subjects are covered in section 8.

However companies seeking a Stock Exchange quotation for the first time can 'go public' in a number of ways and such flotations, as they are termed, often attract a good deal of interest from prospective investors. This is, perhaps, not surprising, since it is not unusual for new company issues to command a market price well above the issue price immediately dealings commence in the open market. 'Stagging' new issues traditionally has been an accepted practice, but professional stags, with their suitcases full of application forms, have today got the process down to a fine art, despite attempts by most issuing houses to reject suspected multiple applications. Add to these the weight of applications from institutional investors – it is not unknown for a single institution to apply for an entire issue – and even the largest issues can be oversubscribed many times. In these circumstances, very large applications normally will be scaled down and those below a certain figure put into a weighted ballot – even if successful in this, applicants for possibly many thousands of shares might be allotted no more than a few hundred.

All this tends to give the impression that the whole new issue process is sometimes little more than a lottery. The problem is that it is not easy to remove the speculative 'froth' without prejudice to the interests of other, genuine, investors, or to the company itself. The escalation in the sheer weight of money seeking new investment opportunities today can also be held partly responsible. Remember that many companies seeking a Stock Exchange listing are expanding, successful ones and so it is not altogether surprising that large numbers of investors often wish to become shareholders in them at the outset of their 'public' life. The company itself will naturally want the launch to be a success, rather than an embarrassing flop, which can happen if the issue is mistimed or the terms pitched on what need be only slightly too adventurous terms. However, there is an increasing trend towards issues by tender (see section 9.2) which are less attractive to speculators and reflect more accurately genuine investment demand for a company's shares. See also section 14.1.

9.2 New issue types and terminology

Allotment letter: A temporary deed of title used to allocate stock or shares provisionally to the person named, usually arising from a rights issue or a successful application for a new issue. Nearly all allotment letters issued by UK companies are negotiable documents and being unregistered are renounceable, in whole or part, without further transfer forms. See also 'Rights issue', section 8.2.

Call: The amount of, or balance, money due on nil or partly paid stocks or shares. It should be noted that failure to pay the call on the due date can result in the forfeiture of the stock or shares.

Introduction: An issue procedure employed when no marketing arrangements are necessary, i.e. when a previously unquoted company seeks only a Stock Exchange listing for its shares, rather than to raise capital by the sale of shares to the public.

However, the securities to be introduced must be of such amount and sufficiently widely held to provide adequate marketability after use.

Issuing house: An institution, normally a merchant bank, which advises companies seeking to raise capital on The Stock Exchange and organises the subsequent issue.

Offer by prospectus: The issue of securities by a company direct to the public at a stated price. The prospectus and application form is published in at least two national newspapers although copies are also made available from the brokers and bankers to the issue. As with all new issues, the company and its advisers must try to strike a balance between obtaining the best price for the company's benefit and pitching the terms on a sufficiently attractive basis to interest the public and ensure the success of the issue.

Offer for sale: A similar procedure to an offer by prospectus, the main difference being that an issuing house or broker acquires from the company the securities being issued and then re-offers them to the public, again normally at a stated price. However, a variation is an . . .

Offer for sale by tender: Which fixes only a minimum subscription price. The investor must then decide if a higher price is warranted and subscribe accordingly. The highest tenders receive allocations of the issue, although applications above the striking price (see below) are allocated at the striking price and the excess application money is returned to the subscribers.

Oversubscribed: Term used when the total amount of shares subscribed for by investors in a new issue exceeds the amount on offer.

Example

Issue	Total amount subscribed	Number of times oversubscribed
10 million shares at 50p each to raise £5 million	£15 million for 30 million shares	3 times

It should be noted that the basis of allocation of new stock or shares to applicants following oversubscription is entirely at the issuing body's discretion.

Partly paid: Stock or shares on which only part of the issue price has been paid, with the balance due on a pre-stated date or at the issuer's demand.

Placing: A new issue procedure, often used when relatively small companies go public, involving the issue of securities by the issuing house or broker through the market and to their own clients. This procedure avoids the higher expenses of an offer by prospectus or offer for sale, but is generally allowed only where there is not likely to be significant public demand for the securities. Applications for securities issued in a placing should be made through a broker in the usual way.

Prospectus: The document accompanying a new issue of stock or shares and containing full and detailed information on the issue and the issuing company, as required by The Stock Exchange.

Stag: An investor who applies for a new issue of stock or shares in anticipation of the initial stock market dealing price being higher than the issue price, with the sole intention of realising an immediate profit.

Striking price: The price at which stock or shares issued by tender is allotted to subscribers. Applications below this price will not receive an allotment.

Undersubscribed: Term used when the total amount of money subscribed by investors for a new issue falls below the amount on offer. In such an event subscribers are allotted their applications in full and, if appropriate, the underwriters are called upon to take up the balance.

Underwriting: A guarantee given by a third party or parties (usually institutional investors) that it or they will subscribe for any stock or shares not taken up in the normal course of a new issue, thus assuring the issuer that the required capital sum will be raised.

Section 10

Stock Exchange price and dealing terminology

10.1 'Ex' formats, 'cum' and 'books closed'

The price qualifications 'ex' (without) and 'cum' (with) are used to determine whether buyer or seller is entitled to receive a forthcoming dividend or capital issue. Thus, a price quotation followed by any of the undermentioned ex formats means that *the seller is entitled to keep* the dividend or issue, i.e. the security is sold without entitlement, while, by the same token, *a buyer is not entitled to it.*

XD – Ex dividend *(sometimes ex distribution)*: On the first day of dealing xd (for account settlement securities this is normally the first day of an account), the market price of an equity is adjusted down by an amount roughly equal to the net dividend payable. This does not apply to fixed interest securities since the accrued interest is accounted for separately.

XC – Ex capitalisation: On the first day of dealing xc (normally the first day of an account) the market price of the shares is adjusted proportionately, to reflect the additional shares in issue (see Example 1 overleaf).

XR – Ex rights: On the first day of dealing xr the market price of the shares is adjusted to reflect the terms of the issue and the premium on the new shares, in nil paid form, will relate to that adjusted price, the call normally being due well after the ex rights date (see Example 2 overleaf).

Example 1

Share price before (or cum) capitalisation issue	Issue basis	Share price after (or ex) capitalisation issue
400p	3 new shares for every 5 held	250p xc

i.e. $$\frac{5 \text{ shares held} \times 400p}{5 \text{ shares held} + 3 \text{ new shares}} = \frac{\pounds 20}{8 \text{ shares}} = 250p \text{ per share}$$

Example 2

Share price before (or cum) rights issue	Issue basis	Share price after (or ex) rights issue	Premium on new shares
300p	1 new share for every 4 held 200p per share	280p xr	80p nil paid

i.e. $$\frac{(4 \text{ shares held} \times 300p) + 200p \text{ cash}}{4 \text{ shares held} + 1 \text{ new share}} = \frac{\pounds 14}{5 \text{ shares}}$$
280p per share*

*or 80p premium over the issue price of 200p for the new shares.

XA – Ex all: Used when the underlying security is quoted ex more than one of the foregoing ex formats on the same day.

Cum: A security is said to be cum any of the foregoing events prior to actually being quoted ex. However, this is deemed to be understood in practice and cum as a price qualification is not usually quoted. Obviously, the buyer of a security in cum form is entitled to any subsequent dividends or capital issues and can claim these from the seller. Indeed, it should be noted that all Stock Exchange securities are sold and purchased with all rights attached and under the terms of the sale contract the seller of a security in cum form is required to deliver to the buyer any dividend or capital issue he may receive after the date of sale and before his name is removed from the stock or share register.

Books closed date *('to holders on register date')*: This is the date on which a register of stocks or shares is closed for the distribution of an interest or dividend payment, or a share or other issue, to the holders listed. However, and this is where misunderstanding can often arise, *this date has no direct relevance to Stock Exchange dealings in the underlying security;* it is the ex date which solely determines whether the seller or buyer is entitled to receive the dividend or payment in question. The need for this system arises because of the inevitable time delay in replacing a seller's name with the buyer's name on the holders' register.

Example

A company, whose shares stand at 400p, announces a capitalisation issue of one new share for each existing share held to shareholders on its register on 15th July, i.e. its books will close on that date. The shares are quoted ex capitalisation on 1st August at 200p xc.

Buyers of the shares up to the last dealing day before 1st August would be entitled to the new shares. By the same token, a seller would not be entitled to keep the new shares, despite the fact that his name may have been on the register as a shareholder when the books were closed and he received a certificate for the new shares.

To pursue this a little further, consider the position if sellers prior to the ex date were permitted to keep the new shares, or dividend. In the above case, they would be selling their old shares for 400p and keeping the new shares worth 200p, making a total worth of 600p, while the buyer would be paying 400p for the seller's shares, which would be worth only half that after 1st August. Obviously, on this basis, everyone would wish to sell their shares and nobody would buy before the ex date . . . which means that nobody could sell!

While for illustration purposes the example of a capitalisation issue has been used, exactly the same principle applies in the case of a dividend or other issue. It bears repetition; the books closed date is an irrelevance so far as the transfer of any rights attaching to the underlying security is concerned.

10.2 Other price and dealing terminology

Assented/non-assented: When a stock or share is subject to a current offer of any sort – for example, a takeover bid or conversion of loan stock – there may be two prices quoted: one

assented to the offer, where the seller has accepted, and the other non-assented to the offer, where the seller has taken no action. Care should be taken that any transactions are in the correct form and that, in the case of assented sales, the appropriately completed and signed acceptance documents can be delivered, if required, with the covering certificate and by the relevant date.
Note: Non-assented bargains are often for cash settlement (immediate delivery).

Bargain: A Stock Exchange transaction.

Bear: An investor who sells a stock or share in anticipation of a fall in the price. It follows that 'bearish' is indicative of pessimism and that a 'bear market' describes a falling trend in share prices.

Bearer securities: Non-registered securities transferable by physical delivery to the buyer and requiring no other transfer documents. Since there is no register of holders of bearer securities, the payment of dividends, etc., is facilitated by numbered coupons attached to the bearer certificate. As each dividend becomes payable, the appropriately numbered coupon must be detached and presented to the company's paying agents. Although most bearer securities are foreign, a few major UK companies have bearer shares in issue, while certain British Government stocks are available in bearer bond form.

Best: The highest bid price or lowest offer price of a security available in the market at the time the order is given.

Bid price: The selling price.

Blue chip: A leading company or its ordinary shares.

Bull: An investor who buys a stock or share in the expectation that its price will rise and therefore produce a capital profit. Most private investors can therefore be said to be 'long-term bulls'! Similarly, 'bullish' indicates optimism about a share or the market and a 'bull market' is one showing a rising trend in prices.

Close price: A narrow spread between bid and offered prices.

Common stock: The main American equivalent of UK ordinary shares.

Discount: Depending on the context in which it is used, indicates that a price quoted for a stock or share is *below* (i) par or maturity value (fixed-interest securities), (ii) the prevailing market price or net asset value (ordinary shares) or (iii) the issue price (new issues).

Limit orders: These involve the placing of an order at a specific maximum (purchases) or minimum (sales) price at which the investor wishes to deal in a particular security. A buying limit will be below, while selling limits must be above, the prevailing market price. This seemingly obvious point is made because 'stop-loss' orders (see page 75) are unacceptable in the London market. It is normal for a broker to retain an impracticable limit order for a period of one month or so, after which it is reviewed. Most brokers will accept only realistic limit orders – typically within a 10% margin of the share price – while normally the capital sum involved should also be of a reasonable size. Monitoring limit orders does involve a fair amount of administration and an absence of regulations of the foregoing nature could easily lead to a broker being inundated with totally unrealistic limit orders.

Marketable amount: An indication of the amount of stock in which it is possible to deal at a quoted price.

Marking names (American and Canadian shares): *Good* or *recognised* marking names are those organisations which appear on The Stock Exchange list of marking names. These bodies have given certain undertakings facilitating the payment of dividends on, and transfer of ownership of, American and Canadian shares. *Bad names* – normally private individuals – are those holders which do not appear in the above list. It should be noted that price quotations for shares in bad names are normally somewhat wider and it is sensible to have such holdings transferred to a recognised name even though this may involve some small expense.

Middle price: A price halfway between the bid and offer prices.

Narrow market: Indicates that it is difficult to deal in a stock or share at the prevailing market price, other than in small amounts.

No par value (NPV): American or Canadian shares which do not have a nominal par value. UK company law prohibits British companies from issuing shares of this nature, although the par value of a share is of little consequence in its ultimate stock market valuation.

Offer price: The buying price.

Par: The face or nominal value of a security. A price given as par is equivalent to this value.

Premium: Depending on the context in which it is used, indicates that a price quoted for a stock or share is *above* (i) par or maturity value (fixed interest securities), (ii) the prevailing market price or net asset value (ordinary shares) or (iii) the issue price (new issue). The *nil paid* premium is the market price of new shares issued by way of rights and on which the call has not fallen due for payment (see section 8.2). An option price is also sometimes referred to as the premium (i.e. the premium over the share price).

Public limited company (PLC): There are some 800,000 companies registered in the UK, of which around 8,000, or 1%, are public limited companies and the remainder private companies. A PLC has the right to issue shares or loan capital to the public at large; a private company does not. Note that the distinction between the two is not the same as between Stock Exchange listed and non-listed companies (there are around 2,300 UK companies listed on The London Stock Exchange).

Quotation suspended: Indicates that the official listing of the security on The Stock Exchange has been temporarily withdrawn and no dealings can take place. It does not mean that the security is valueless as a share may well be suspended prior to an important and possibly beneficial announcement. *Quotation cancelled* would indicate the listing to have been permanently withdrawn.

Selling uncovered (*or selling short*): A form of dealing which most broking firms will not accept. It involves the sale of securities not actually owned by the seller, who takes the view that the price will drop, thus enabling him to repurchase them at a lower price, usually in the same Stock Exchange account. Obviously, this amounts to outright speculation and the losses which can accrue in the event of the judgement being wrong and the share price rising can be considerable – indeed, theoretically, unlimited.

Size: The amount of stock or shares in which the market maker is making the price quoted; the quote often widens for very large amounts.

Stop-loss orders: No facilities exist within the London market for accepting American-style stop-loss orders, the principle of which involves setting a firm selling price below the prevailing market price in order to limit a loss on an investment.

Touch: The closest price quotation in a security between different market makers, i.e. the best bid and cheapest offer prices available in the market.

Wide price: A wider than average spread between the bid and offered prices.

10.3 Probate prices and valuations

Valuations of Stock Exchange securities for probate purposes are based on prices from *The Stock Exchange Daily Official List* for the date of death. The basis of valuation is (i) the bid price plus one-quarter of the difference between the bid and offered prices, or (ii) halfway between the lowest and highest marks, whichever is the lower.

Example

SEDOL quote	Marks	Probate price
100–120p	106, 8, 10	105p
300–350p	300, 320, 315	310p

When death occurs on a Saturday, Sunday or bank holiday, the valuation can be based on prices ruling on either the last preceding or the first succeeding Stock Exchange business day.

It should be noted that account must be taken of dividends or capital issues if the quotation is succeeded by any 'ex' format (see section 10.1).

Section 11

Managed investment funds

11.1 General comments

A managed investment fund in this context is one which offers investors a means of participation in a particular financial market or sector via a portfolio of investments which is under constant professional supervision. The fund will be one of two types – *open end,* such as a unit trust, or *closed end,* such as an investment trust company. These terms reflect the different structure of the two types of fund which are explained further in sections 11.2 and 11.4.

The advantages of managed funds to private investors – and not just those with limited resources – are considerable:

i   They provide a much broader market coverage within a single investment than most private investors are able to achieve economically through a portfolio of 'individual' holdings.

ii By virtue of (i), the risk element, especially in equity funds, is reduced to a minimum.

iii The underlying portfolio is managed by experts in the particular area covered, on a much more active basis than are most private portfolios.

iv There can be tax advantages. For example, authorised unit trusts and recognised investment trusts are exempt from tax on their capital gains (although, of course, transactions in the units or shares by investors are assessable to capital gains tax in the normal way – see section S2).

v   They tend to require less administration than a portfolio of individual stocks and shares.

vi   Most funds keep their unit- or shareholders in touch with the progress of the underlying portfolio via a six-monthly report.

There is now a vast range of funds available covering the United Kingdom and the most important overseas markets, from a broad to a highly specialised basis. You can buy funds for income and funds for capital growth – or a compromise between the two. There are funds invested in gilts, in international bonds, in foreign currencies and in sterling deposits. For most private investors seeking to invest in overseas markets – for example, the United States, Japan, Hong Kong, Australia, Malaysia and Singapore or Continental Europe – either individually or on a diversified basis, a managed fund can usually be recommended. Apart from a wide choice of broadly based equity funds, there are those which specialise in the shares of companies involved in particular industries or sectors, such as natural resources, high technology, finance and property. There are even funds of funds – unit trusts invested in the shares of investment trust companies. Others concentrate on smaller companies and higher-risk 'recovery stocks' and 'special situations'. At least one fund is invested exclusively in shares traded on the Unlisted Securities Market and another specialises in 'penny' shares.

This wide choice means that it is possible to construct, from managed funds alone, a balanced portfolio which contains a high degree of diversification, yet which is compact and easily supervised. Indeed, with so much apparently in their favour, why do so many people still prefer to concentrate on individual stocks and shares? There are a number of reasons for this. One is that many investors are 'locked in' long-standing portfolios by capital gains tax considerations and, anyway, are often set firmly in their investment ways. It must be remembered that, although many quoted investment trust companies have a long history and the first unit trusts appeared in the 1930s, the managed fund concept with all its highly sophisticated derivatives has proliferated only within recent years. For many UK investors, too, a direct purchase of British Government securities is often seen as preferable to a managed gilt fund because of the capital gains tax advantage of the former.

However, the main reason why managed *equity* funds do not appeal to many investors is that they take the 'spice' out of the equity investment equation. Despite the fact that many fund management groups can point to outstanding and consistent records of achievement, investing in this medium does not provide that sense of participation and anticipation which can be felt by watching the progress of 'your' company. Certainly, it virtually eliminates any chance of the sort of spectacular price action that is sometimes seen in the stock market, for example, as a result of takeover bid activity. Moreover, that not all investors should be attracted exclusively to managed funds is a desirable factor in the maintenance of a competitive market.

None the less, there is a definite trend towards a wider use of managed funds in private investment portfolios, especially as a means of achieving representation of overseas markets or a particular sector. By definition, the decision as to which shares to buy and which to sell is left to the fund managers, but the investor still has to choose the fund or funds at the outset and, indeed, must be prepared to swap them around from time to time to reflect changes in the prevailing investment climate.

As ever, seek unbiased professional guidance in the first place and have your holdings reviewed at least once a year. Do not choose your investment haphazardly, for example on the basis of the most enticing advertisement in the Sunday papers or simply because it happened to be 'last year's best-performing fund . . .' (it is not unknown for one year's best performer to be amongst the next year's worst and vice versa). Equally, however, don't be fobbed off with an adviser's 'in-house' fund (see section 11.5) without reasonable evidence that it stands up to comparison with independently managed funds, or if you feel that it does not entirely meet your objectives. Otherwise, the best advice is to keep to well-known management groups which can point to records of consistent achievement over their whole fund range, which in turn should not be too small or too diverse.

11.2 Investment trusts

An investment trust is an ordinary limited company in which the investor can buy shares on The Stock Exchange in the normal way. It is an example of a *closed end* fund – a term which refers to its fixed capital structure, the market value of which is determined by supply and demand in accordance with the influences discussed in section 7.2 although in turn this will be governed largely by the trust's performance figures, i.e. the rate of growth achieved in net asset value and dividends paid to shareholders. Two of the major attractions of investment trust shares, which can work to shareholders' advantage in periods of prolonged market strength, and vice versa, are as follows:

i   Unlike unit trusts, most can be purchased at a discount to their net asset value. (This discount is usually expressed as a percentage of the net asset value figure.) It should be noted that discount levels can fluctuate, reflecting market conditions and the supply of and demand for the shares in question but, in recent years, only a few 'special situation' investment trusts have stood at a premium to their net asset value.

ii Gearing (see section 8.4) can be introduced by raising fixed interest capital for investment purposes and, hopefully, the appreciation of and income from the investments purchased with the money borrowed will in due course service the loan and leave a residue for the benefit of ordinary shareholders.

11.3 Split-capital investment trusts

The ordinary share capital of split-capital investment trusts is divided into two classes, usually designated *income* and *capital* shares. Unlike orthodox investment trusts, most have a fixed life, at the end of which the trust is put into voluntary liquidation. During the life of the trust the income shares receive, by way of dividends, all the income earned by its underlying investments and on liquidation are repaid at a predetermined price which, it should be noted, may well be less than the prevailing market price of the shares. The capital shares are paid no – or only nominal – dividends but are usually entitled to all the proceeds of the ultimate liquidation, less only the amount required to repay the income shares. They can, therefore, be attractive to higher-rate taxpayers or anyone to whom capital growth is the sole investment objective.

11.4 Unit trusts

A unit trust is not a company; it is simply a portfolio of investments in which investors can buy or sell units. It is *open ended* which means that it has no fixed capital but issues and cancels units – each unit being a proportionate share – as investors buy and sell. Note that for this reason supply and demand play no part in the price of the units. The portfolio is administered by a management company, which makes its profit by predetermined charges on the fund – typically an initial charge of 5% with an annual charge of perhaps 1% of its capital value – and by handling the buying and selling of units. Otherwise, it has no access to the capital invested by the public; indeed, trustees, normally an insurance company or a bank, are appointed to hold the assets of the fund in safe keeping. Unit trust prices are based on the exact asset value per unit, which is calculated by reference to the total net market value of the fund and dividing this by the number of units in issue. To this is added or deducted a sum, calculated by a formula laid down by the Board of Trade, to arrive at the bid and offered prices respectively. Most unit trusts are valued on a daily basis; a few, usually less widely held trusts, not so frequently.

A feature of many unit trusts is that income distributions, at the holder's election, may be automatically reinvested in further units, a facility which can be particularly useful when, for example, investing money for minors. Such units are termed *accumulation units*, but it should be noted that the notional income reinvested is treated as investment income in the normal manner and taxed accordingly.

In practical terms, unit trusts are probably a good medium for private investors seeking a diversified exposure to equity markets, especially overseas markets, although this is not to discourage those who really want to be direct shareholders in industry and commerce from doing so. The answer is normally a compromise between the two; by all means hold shares in a range of leading companies – and even have a flutter here and there in something a little more speculative – but supplement these with some unit trusts to give your portfolio breadth and geographical diversification.

Certainly, it seems likely that the advantages of unit trusts will continue to gain increasing recognition among investors, a view given added support by the fact that unit trust holders do not have to be concerned with rights issues, capitalisation issues, takeovers and other events which can make capital gains tax computations such a daunting task. This having been said, it is debatable whether gilt-edged unit trusts have a real advantage over a well-selected range of, say, three or four individual stocks. To repeat a point emphasised throughout this section – get good independent advice, or even take a second opinion if in doubt, before making any major decisions.

11.5 In-house funds

This is the popular name given to investment funds – usually unit trusts – set up and managed internally by stockbrokers, banks and other investment houses for the particular benefit of their own clients or customers, although many are made available to 'outside' investors as well.

Indeed some organisations now insist that smaller portfolios under their management include investments in their own funds; others may reduce management fees if their funds are held. This is not necessarily a bad thing, given the advantages of managed funds to the smaller investor, especially if you know and trust the organisation concerned. However, seek a second opinion if you are not convinced that what is being proposed for your investments is in your best interest. This can be especially important if you are considering a share exchange scheme, under which you are offered units in a managed fund, normally a unit trust, in exchange for your holdings of stocks and shares. Watch out for capital gains tax (you will not always get advice on this), don't get left with any poorer-quality or small holdings just because the management company doesn't want them and perhaps be just a little wary of the adviser who tells you to put everything into one company's range of funds or other products: he *may* be right, but variety is, after all, the spice of investment life.

The Financial Services Bill proposes that all investment advisers should disclose to clients any connection between themselves and in-house funds which they recommend, a rule which applied to Stock Exchange member firms with effect from 27th October 1986.

11.6 Offshore funds

An offshore fund is one which is based in countries or principalities with 'favourable' local tax legislation, usually allowing the fund to operate without tax on its income or capital. Places which have a thriving financial community for this very reason are the Bahamas, Bermuda, the Cayman Islands and, nearer to home, the Isle of Man. However, the doyens of the offshore fund industry, at least as far as the UK investment markets are concerned, are the Channel Islands. Nearly all the major UK investment houses and banks now have offices in Jersey or Guernsey, offering a range of managed funds and other financial services. Originally, these were aimed at the expatriate market – those investors who live or work abroad but wish to leave their capital in a tax-efficient yet stable environment and, in the case of the Channel Islands, on the 'doorstep' of the United Kingdom.

None the less, there is today a rapidly growing range of investment vehicles designed as much for the UK investor as the expatriate, especially in the relatively new field of 'money' or 'currency' funds (but see section 11.7). These apart, for UK investors offshore funds offer no great advantage or disadvantage over mainland-based funds except, perhaps, in respect of gilt-edged funds (which is why there are more such funds offshore than 'onshore'). For non-resident investors they will almost certainly be a more worthwhile proposition than mainland-based funds – and, indeed, many other types of investment – exposed to a more punitive tax legislation.

It should be noted that offshore funds do not come under the control of the Department of Trade and thus are not required to comply with the regulations governing, for example, mainland-based unit trusts. However, to prevent, as far as possible, misrepresentation, or even fraud, there are severe restrictions on the marketing of offshore funds in the United Kingdom. Moreover, the Channel Islands authorities, in particular, impose their own stringent conditions upon organisations seeking to launch funds locally. As always, the best policy is to go for funds offered by well-known institutions with a proven record in investment fund management.

11.7 Currency funds

The concept behind currency funds is simplicity itself; the resources of a large number of small investors are pooled to create sums large enough to trade competitively in money market deposits and instruments. By virtue of their offshore locations (see section 11.6) the income accruing to the fund can be distributed to its investors or reinvested *on a gross basis*.

Funds are available in most major currencies including the US dollar, Japanese yen, German Deutschmark and Swiss franc; in a number of more minor currencies; and, of course, in sterling. There are also composite funds where the choice of currencies held is left to the discretion of the managers. Most invest on a very short-term basis, ranging mainly from 'overnight' to three months. This provides the fund with a high degree of liquidity, and settlement of transactions in the underlying shares or units is normally two days after dealing. The charges levied by the managers are much lower than conventionally managed funds, for example gilt or equity funds, amounting usually to no more than a small charge against the interest receivable; also most trade on a single price basis.

Funds invested in *foreign* currencies have a number of applications. Private individuals can hold them as short- or long-term investments, depending upon the strategy being employed. Small businesses can use them to hedge their currency commitments. In short they open up foreign exchange markets to smaller investors on an economic scale. However, it is always a two-way bet. The risk remains that rates will move against the investor – in this specific context, that sterling will strengthen against the chosen currency – and if the movement is large enough it can more than eliminate the value of the interest accrued. Many people do not want to expose themselves to such a risk and, anyway, what could be more sensible than an equivalent fund in sterling for foreign investors or as a 'bolthole' for UK residents during periods of strength in the pound?

These funds – especially sterling funds – proved popular with investors liable to higher rates of UK tax during the early 1980s because of the advantage inherent in 'capitalising income' in the above way. However, the Government closed this 'loophole' with legislation which became effective from 1st January 1984. Capital gains realised on such funds after that date become chargeable to income tax, except where the fund has 'distributor' status, i.e. it distributes its income to its investors by way of dividends, instead of rolling it up in the price.

Section 12

Insurance-linked (single premium) bonds

Although insurance-linked bonds are not Stock Exchange securities as such, they are solely designed for the private investment sector and are actively marketed. Investors should take advice from an independent professional source before committing their capital to a specific bond.

12.1 General comments

A bond in this context is a single premium (lump sum) life policy linked to a unit fund and the bond's value is measured by the performance of the fund. Thus, the premium is used to purchase units in the chosen fund at the prevailing price, which is arrived at in a similar manner to that described for unit trusts in section 11.4. The bonds are purchased and surrendered through the management companies in much the same way as unit trusts, while there is also a similar management charge structure. Bondholders receive no annual interest or dividends, any income earned by the underlying investments being retained in the fund. This, together with their tax treatment (see section 12.2), makes bonds of this type primarily attractive to higher-rate taxpayers seeking to reduce or minimise their tax liabilities. Generally speaking, they have not proved that these benefits outweigh those of more traditional investment areas for investors liable to no more than standard-rate income tax, or those with limited capital resources.

12.2 The tax treatment of bonds

While life insurance companies do enjoy certain tax concessions which can be passed on to bondholders, the underlying fund is nevertheless liable to tax on both its income and capital gains. However, since the bonds are technically life insurance policies they are exempt from capital gains tax and basic-rate income tax in the hands of the investor, the only tax consideration being the possibility of a liability to higher rates of income tax when encashed.

The liability is calculated on a 'top-slicing' basis by dividing the capital gain by the number of complete years the bond has been in force. The resultant figure is regarded as income and treated as if it were the top slice of the bondholder's income in the year of encashment. The average tax rate on this 'slice', less the basic income tax rate, is then applied to the whole gain to arrive at the total tax liability.

In the case of partial encashments of 5% or less per annum of the sum invested, which includes regular withdrawal plans, the tax assessment is deferred until the bond is finally surrendered. This annual 5% 'allowance' works on a cumulative basis up to a total of 100%, the limit being 20 years, at which point there would be a tax assessment on the basis described above. If the cumulative annual allowance is exceeded at any point, an immediate assessment will be made.

While bonds of this type can be tax efficient vehicles for high-rate taxpayers, it is clearly desirable to plan any such investments in the light of the investor's anticipated circumstances and tax position. Hence the recommendation at the beginning of this section that prospective bond investors firstly consult a reliable advisory source.

12.3 Bond types

There is now a wide choice of bonds available linked to unit funds invested in property, equities, fixed-interest securities and cash deposits or a combination of these. Individual management groups usually offer their own range covering all these sectors, often with facilities to switch between funds on advantageous terms in accordance with the bondholder's judgement of market conditions (the management company will normally offer no advice on the timing of these switches, the decisions being left to the investor or his advisers). A brief summary of the five principal types of bond is given below:

Cash, money or convertible bonds: These bonds are invested in cash deposits or near-cash securities and are primarily designed as a temporary investment vehicle for high-rate taxpayers (the interest received by the fund is effectively converted into capital, which, in turn, is reflected in the unit price) or for those investors who believe property and/or equity values might fall in the short term, thus presenting an opportunity to convert or switch back into bonds within the same management group and linked to these latter markets at lower unit price levels.

Equity bonds: These are bonds linked to a unit fund invested in ordinary shares, either directly or through the medium of an ordinary unit trust under the same management roof. Apart from the addition of the modest life assurance element, there is little difference between an equity bond and a conventional unit trust, but for many investors, particularly those who have no liability to higher rates of income tax, conventional unit trusts offer an equally good choice of funds and can have certain other advantages. The most important of these is that unit trusts are themselves effectively exempt from tax on their capital gains, whereas bond funds are not. It is true that, conversely, gains established on a sale of unit trust units by the investor are assessable to capital gains tax, whereas bonds surrendered are not. However, where gains on unit trusts are kept within the annual CGT 'exempt' limit (see section S2), they will also effectively be tax free.

Fixed-interest bonds: As their title implies, these bonds are invested primarily in fixed-interest securities such as Government stocks, local authority issues, fixed-term deposits, etc., and, as with 'cash' bonds mentioned above, can have attractions for higher-rate taxpayers in that the income received by the fund is effectively converted into capital. Some investors might find that a direct investment in the gilt-edged market, with its associated capital gains tax advantages would be more suitable, but, of course, a bond does offer professional management on a day-to-day basis.

Managed bonds: This is the general description given to the type of bond which encompasses an interest in property, equities and fixed-interest stocks in a single bond investment. The proportions invested in any one sector can vary and are at the discretion of the managers, depending on their assessment of market conditions. Clearly, these bonds are designed for the investor who does not wish to be actively involved in the management of his capital.

Property bonds: This is the most widely held type of investment bond, possibly because there is no other easily accessible investment available which enables the investor to take a direct interest in commercial property ownership, short of buying a property outright – and office blocks or industrial estates are beyond the means of most private investors. The majority of property bond funds invest in commercial and industrial properties: however, funds concentrating on agricultural and forestry land are available. It should be noted that most funds maintain a fairly high element of liquidity to meet encashments, etc., so that the 'property' interest is diluted somewhat. The important point to understand here is that the value of property bond funds is linked to the *estimated* market value of the underlying properties, in much the same way as a unit trust price is linked to the value of its stock market investments; on the other hand, share prices of property companies are subject to the normal influences discussed in section 7.2, but can frequently be purchased at good discounts to their estimated net asset value which will, of course, essentially reflect the value of their properties.

12.4 Withdrawal facilities

These enable bondholders to obtain an 'income' from their investment by withdrawing a predetermined percentage of the original investment each year. Provided this does not exceed 5% of the sum invested there is no year-on-year tax liability (but see section 12.2). Income in this sense is a slight misnomer, as the cash is provided by the sale, at the ruling price, of sufficient of the bondholder's units to produce the sum required (although it can be regarded as a form of access to the reinvested income in the fund). Nevertheless, the bondholder is essentially eating into capital to provide an income and, unless the underlying units appreciate in price by an equivalent amount between withdrawals, the bond value will gradually diminish. Indeed, if the unit price drops significantly, owing to market trends, the compounding effects of a withdrawal facility can be severe. This having been said, there can be no doubt that withdrawal schemes can be immensely valuable to high-rate taxpayers who find a need to supplement their income and for this category of investor, bonds having a withdrawal facility can fulfil a useful role in investment planning.

Section 13
Options and warrants

13.1 Conventional (non-traded) options

There are three forms of conventional option dealing, namely a *call, put* or *double* (or *two-way* or *put-and-call*) option.

A call option entitles the holder to buy shares, within a fixed period of time, at a pre-arranged price (known as the *exercise* or *striking price*), which will be much in line with the market price of the shares when the option is taken out. Call options are thus of interest to investors who believe the price of a share will rise during that period. Conversely, a put option entitles the holder to sell shares on the same basis and is therefore taken out if a fall in the share price is anticipated. A double option encompasses both and allows the holder to buy or sell the shares, depending on which way the price moves. However, as might be expected, a double costs about twice as much as a single call or put option.

The normal option period is three months and the holder can exercise the option at any time within that period. However, one-month options can sometimes be arranged, these being somewhat cheaper than three-month options. If the underlying share price does not move as expected, the option is abandoned. Thus, the potential loss on an option is limited to the initial cost; the significance of this is illustrated by the example overleaf.

The price of an option depends on three main factors: the underlying share price level, its marketability and its volatility. However, as a rough guide, most option prices tend to be between 5% and 15% of the share price, plus expenses.

Example

Suppose an investor believes that the shares of ABC PLC, standing at 200p in the market, will rise to 250p in the near future and has £4,000 available for investment. The three-month call option price is 20p, with an exercise price of 200p. He could:

  i   Buy 2,000 shares outright, cost £4,000.
 ii   Limit the risk, i.e. the equity exposure, by taking out a call option in 2,000 shares, cost £400, and investing the balance of his £4,000 elsewhere to earn interest in the meantime.
iii   If extremely adventurous, increase the risk by taking out a call option in 20,000 shares at a cost of the full £4,000, thus introducing a considerable element of equity 'gearing'.

Clearly, the underlying shares must rise by over 20p to guarantee the investor a profit in cases (ii) and (iii). The following table shows the position of the alternatives in the event of (a) the anticipated share price action materialising and (b), against the investor's expectation, the price falling to 150p at the expiry date.

Share price at expiry		
250p		150p
i	Realisable profit £1,000 (2,000 shares @ 50p). Alternatively, the shares could be retained.	Realisable loss £1,000 (2,000 shares @ 50p). Alternatively, the shares could be retained for recovery.
ii	Realisable profit of £600 (2,000 shares called and sold at 50p profit = £1,000, less £400 option money) plus interest on £3,600. Shares could be called and retained at additional cost of £4,000.	Loss of £400 option money, less interest on £3,600.
iii	Realisable profit of £6,000 (20,000 shares called and sold at 50p profit = £10,000, less £4,000 option money). Shares could be called and retained at additional cost of £40,000.	Loss of £4,000 option money.

Note: Expenses excluded throughout.

Options can be arranged only if another investor is prepared to act as the *writer* of the option, although in practice this rarely presents any difficulty. The writer, normally an institutional investor, receives the option money in exchange for an undertaking to sell the underlying shares to a call option holder, or buy the shares from a put option holder, at the exercise price. The writer is therefore adopting a contrary strategy to the option holder.

As far as costs are concerned, commission plus VAT is normally charged immediately. The commission is usually calculated on a consideration based on the full exercise price, as if the option had been exercised, not on the option money. Government stamp duty is charged if, and when, the option is exercised.

Note: The *Financial Times* publishes a representative list of three-month call option rates under its Share Information Service.

13.2 Traded options

The London Traded Options Market was opened in April 1978. The *modus operandi* and terminology of this market are complex and it is not possible to cover the subject in detail in this publication. Nevertheless, the following summary should provide an insight to the principles behind traded options.

The traded options market takes the concept of a conventional *call* or *put* option (see section 13.1), imposes various refinements and standardisations and makes the option itself transferable, i.e. tradable, during its life. At the time of writing, traded options are available on 42 active leading shares. In addition, options on two gilt-edged stocks and the Financial Times/Stock Exchange 100 Share Index have been introduced.

Traded options have a maximum life of nine months, arranged on a three-month cycle so that there are always three expiry dates available. When the shortest option expires, a new nine-month option is created. On the introduction of an option for the first time, a range of up to three *exercise* prices (see section 13.1) is created for each expiry date. If the share price moves above the highest, or below the lowest, a new option will be created, so that at any one time there could be five or six exercise prices available for each of the three expiry dates. All options on a particular company's shares are known as a *class* and each of the different options within a class is termed a *series*.

The market price of a traded option is made up of two parts: an *intrinsic value* which exists only if the share price is higher (call option) or lower (put option) than the exercise price, and a gradually diminishing *time value,* which reflects the time remaining before the option expires. The dealing unit is a *contract* which normally represents 1,000 shares.

Example

Suppose it is January and traded call options are to be introduced on the shares of ABC PLC, the market price of the shares being 200p. The following options might be created:

Options class: ABC PLC

Option series (expiry date and exercise price)	Opening offer price of call option p	Effective price paid for shares p
April 180	27 (20 intrinsic + 7 time)	207
April 200	12 (all time)	212
April 220	4 (all time)	224
July 180	32 (20 intrinsic + 12 time)	212
July 200	18 (all time)	218
July 220	9 (all time)	229
October 180	36 (20 intrinsic + 16 time)	216
October 200	23 (all time)	223
October 220	13 (all time)	233

A typical dealing instruction would be given as 'Buy 5 contracts ABC July 200s' (costing 5,000 × 18p = £900, plus expenses).

As might be expected, the longer the option period, the higher the price of those series with the same exercise price, but the obvious question when faced with so many 'options' is, 'Which one do I buy?' This will depend on a number of factors, but it is probably best to illustrate the basic pros and cons by considering the ultimate effect of various underlying share price actions on different option series.

Example

Extracting the three April series of ABC PLC, as above, the following table shows the position at the April expiry date in the event of three different movements in the underlying share price:

Option series	Opening offer price p	Change in opening offer price with share price at expiry:		
		190p	220p	250p
April 180	27	− 17(63%)	+ 13(48%)	+ 43(159%)
April 200	12	− 12(100%)	+ 8(67%)	+ 38(317%)
April 220	4	− 4(100%)	− 4(100%)	+ 26(650%)

+ = Profit.
− = Loss.
Note: Expenses excluded.

The conclusion that can be drawn from this example is that purchasing traded options with a partly intrinsic value (e.g. April 180s) gives a lower risk/reward ratio and is therefore the most conservative strategy, despite involving a greater cash commitment, while those having only time value (e.g. April 220s) offer a high risk/reward ratio and are the most speculative, although the initial cash outlay can be relatively small. Obviously, the buyer of a traded call option will essentially be taking the view that the underlying shares will rise in price during its life. On the other hand, the buyer of a traded put option acquires the right to sell shares at the exercise price, and so a fall in the share price will increase the value of that right and hence the value − price − of the option, and vice versa.

Unlike conventional options, traded options by definition are not linked to one specific *writer* (see section 13.1). Thus, an investor can become a writer, i.e. adopt a contrary strategy to the option buyer, simply by selling a traded call or put option without a previous purchase. However, writers of traded options incur certain liabilities and are required to provide security in respect of the options written. Writing traded options is a strategy which should be undertaken only by those investors who have acquired a complete understanding of this market.

Any position taken in traded options by either buyer or writer can be neutralised by making a contra or closing transaction before the expiry date. Special commission rates apply to traded options; interested investors can obtain these from their broker. Traded options are treated as cash bargains.

The Stock Exchange has published a booklet containing detailed information on traded options, the associated terminology and the numerous investment applications they offer. It can be obtained free of charge from the Information and Press Department of The Stock Exchange (address on page 184).

13.3 A summary of options

Both conventional options and traded options are highly specialised markets and are essentially – but not exclusively – of interest to the professional investor who can apply the use of options to a number of different investment strategies which are beyond the scope of this guide.

The type of private investor to whom options may be of interest is the individual who takes an active and knowledgeable interest in his investments and stock market trends generally and who is prepared to accept the high risk/reward ratio of options. However, most will find options too speculative.

The two categories of options covered in sections 13.1 and 13.2 should not be confused with *registered share options* issued by companies which have a Stock Exchange quotation. These resemble warrants, as described in section 13.4 below.

13.4 Warrants

Quoted warrants are, in effect, registered long-term call options. They entitle holders to buy shares in a company at a fixed subscription price during a specified period of time which often runs into several years. As with call options, therefore, they are of interest to investors who believe the underlying ordinary shares will rise in price during the subscription period, involve a measure of risk and pay no annual dividends. Holders have no rights whatever beyond those defined by the subscription terms and in the event of the share price falling below the warrant subscription price for the whole of the remaining subscription period, the warrants are rendered valueless. So, before exercising their subscription rights, warrant holders should satisfy themselves that the prevailing share price exceeds the subscription price.

What can make warrants attractive is that having established a price relationship with the ordinary shares the warrant price can be expected to move more or less in line with the ordinary shares. This means that a similar price rise in both, in money terms, will represent a greater percentage gain on the (lower) warrant price than on the ordinary shares. Warrants can therefore present the opportunity to introduce long-term equity 'gearing' to an investment, as options do in the short term. The call option example in section 13.1 can be used to illustrate this.

Section 14
Unlisted securities

14.1 The Unlisted Securities Market (USM)

The Unlisted Securities Market, inaugurated in November 1980, essentially provides a regulated secondary market for the shares of small companies which do not meet the requirements for a full quotation laid down by The Stock Exchange. In this way, small or new companies wishing to raise equity capital have access to the stock market 'machinery', while the investor is able to participate in a company's development at an early stage.

Companies quoted on the USM do have to meet certain conditions to enable a degree of regulation to be achieved; however, by virtue of its very purpose, these are considerably less rigid and exhaustive than those admitting a company to full quotation (although there are similar 'continuing disclosure' rules). This is particularly true of UK-domiciled mineral exploration companies or 'less mature' companies seeking finance to put fully researched projects into operation, where, in both cases, certain additional dispensations may apply. The point here is that the USM represents the 'grass-roots' end of the stock market and as such the risk/reward ratio must be accepted as much higher; this apart, the number of shares traded is usually small (only 10% of a company's equity capital need be in public hands, compared with 25% in the case of a company with a full listing) which, in turn, may mean limited marketability and a potentially volatile price action.

Inevitably, many of these companies operate in expanding,

but often cash-hungry, 'high-tech' industries and, with demand for such investment opportunities seemingly insatiable, the premiums over their issue prices rapidly commanded by many USM shares often puts them on to substantially forward-looking ratings in terms of dividend yields (if any) and price/earnings ratios. This makes the shares vulnerable to a turn in sentiment or a failure by the company to live up to expectations. In such cases the marketability factor is an important one. With perhaps only 10% of a company's shares freely traded, price movements can be exaggerated by a flood of simultaneous orders which will often follow, for example, press comment on a share. Investors alerted to shares 'tipped' in this way should be wary of 'chasing' the price to substantially higher levels. It is normally best to check the price before dealing and, if it is well up, to wait a few days in case a better buying opportunity occurs after the dust has settled; it frequently does. Remember, market makers read newspapers, too, and know just what to expect when a particular share receives favourable (or unfavourable) comment in the City pages!

All in all, shares traded on the USM generally carry more risk. Indeed, all contract notes issued by members of The Stock Exchange in respect of transactions in shares quoted on the USM must bear the following statement:

'This security is not listed on The Stock Exchange and the company has not been subjected to the same degree of regulation as a listed security.'

14.2 'Rule 535' transactions

Stock Exchange Rule 535 covers the securities in which members are permitted to deal. However, investors will often hear a security referred to as a '535 stock'; used in this context, it usually means a security (generally an equity) which does not have a full Stock Exchange listing or is not quoted on the Unlisted Securities Market.

The relevant provisions are as under:

Rule 535(2): This covers dealings in UK securities not listed on any stock exchange. The purpose of this provision is to facilitate 'occasional' transactions in the securities of (usually small) companies which have not attained full listing status. Companies whose shares are traded under this rule are not subject to any listing requirements, although a limited degree of *market* regulation is achieved by the fact that all orders in such securities are *'subject to permission to deal' ('SPD')*. In other words, all transactions have to be sanctioned by The Stock Exchange before a firm bargain can be struck.

All contract notes issued by members of The Stock Exchange in respect of transactions in shares traded under this rule must bear the following statement:

'This security is not listed on any stock exchange and the company is not subject to any listing requirements in the United Kingdom and the Republic of Ireland.'

Rule 535(3): This provision recognises the special character of mineral exploration companies in that without publicly subscribed 'venture capital' such companies may not be able to develop their exploration or production programmes. Securities of approved companies in this field are therefore traded more freely, i.e. are not 'subject to permission to deal'.

Shares dealt in under Rules 535(2) and (3), especially the latter, must, as a general rule, be regarded as speculative, and, while participation in small or new companies is to be encouraged, prospective investors must be prepared to accept a high risk factor in return for the reward they anticipate.

Note:

i   It is by virtue of Rule 535(4)(a) that dealings are permitted in securities quoted or listed on any overseas stock exchange.

ii Saturday editions of the *Financial Times* contain a summary of the previous week's transactions under Rules 535(4)(a), (2) and (3).

14.3 The Third Market

The Third Market, due to be launched in the autumn of 1986, follows in the footsteps of the highly successful 'second tier market', the Unlisted Securities Market (see section 14.1). Its purpose is to provide the public with access to a centralised, regulated, market in the shares of small or young companies whose trading record or other considerations do not qualify them for entry into the USM. By the same token, those companies have the opportunity to take advantage of The Stock Exchange's capital-raising machinery at an even earlier stage of their development than the USM offers.

Companies entering the Third Market will represent a cross-section of the United Kingdom business community. It will include companies seeking a capital injection via a wider shareholder base for the first time and others whose shares are at present traded 'off-market' either under the provisions of Stock Exchange Rule 535.3, as described in section 14.2, or by other licensed share dealers on what is known as the Over The Counter ('OTC') market.

The Third Market is designed to promote investor participation in companies at grass roots level and the shares which will be traded on it must be seen as high-risk investments.

Section 15

Shareholder concessions

The references to specific shareholder concessions in this section are for information purposes only and do not constitute a recommendation to purchase any of the shares or other securities concerned. Prospective buyers should also be aware that concessions are not rights and may be altered, or even withdrawn.

15.1 General comments

The subject of shareholder concessions is one which generates a good deal of interest among investors and it is certainly true that the number of companies offering their shareholders discounts of one sort or another on certain of their products or services is steadily, and laudably, increasing. If utilised, these 'perks' can effectively increase the return on a shareholder's investment.

However, there are one or two points prospective purchasers should bear in mind when considering the shares of a company offering what to them may appear worthwhile concessions. Firstly, the concessions are often of a temporary nature only, i.e. must be utilised by a specific date, and could be withdrawn or altered at any time. Secondly, some companies require shareholders to be registered for a specified period of time and/or to hold a minimum number of shares before they qualify for the concession. Thirdly, and most importantly, the merits of the shares as an investment, based on the usual criteria and considerations, remain a vital consideration.

In principle, therefore, concessions should be seen by investors as they are normally intended by the company; that is to say, as recognition of the fundamental role of the shareholders as owners of the business, and rarely, if ever, as the sole basis for a purchase of shares.

It would be impracticable to include a fully detailed list of shareholder concessions in this guide but there are a few which seem to attract particular interest among investors; consequently details of ten popular concessions are given in section 15.2, while section 15.3 contains a simplified list of 50 other companies which offer their shareholders benefits of various kinds. In both cases, the details given are understood to be accurate as at the publication date of this guide. However, prospective investors can confirm the up-to-date position by reference to the appropriate company secretary or a broker.

15.2 Ten popular concessions

Concession	Qualifying shares (qualifying holding/ registration period)

Barratt Developments
Wingrove House, Ponteland Road,
Newcastle upon Tyne NE5 3DP

Price reduction on new Barratt house	Ordinary 10p (1,000 on reg. for 1 year)

European Ferries
PO Box 12, 1 Camden Crescent, Dover, Kent CT16 1LD

Discounts on Townsend Thoresen ferry rates: 50% on Dover to Calais/Zeebrugge route, 50% on Felixstowe/Zeebrugge route, 40% on Southampton/Portsmouth to Cherbourg or Le Havre route, 25% on Cairnryan to Larne route. Covers car and up to four adult passengers but not towed caravans. No limit on number of crossings but certain restrictions at peak times.	5% Cum. Pref. (600)

Grand Metropolitan
Grand Metropolitan House, 7/8 Stratford Place,
London W1A 4YU

Various discounts on wines and spirits. 10% discount on 'mini-holidays'. Vouchers towards meals at certain group restaurants.	Ordinary 25p (No minimum)

Concession	Qualifying shares (qualifying holding/ registration period)

Horizon Travel
214 Broad Street, Birmingham B15 1BB

10% discount on holidays to a maximum brochure value of £1,000, i.e. maximum discount of £100 (shareholder and party).

Ordinary 5p (750 on reg. for 6 months)

Ladbroke Group
Hanover House, Lyon Road, Harrow, Middlesex HA1 2BR

Principal concessions:
10% discount at group hotels/restaurants.
10% discount on holidays during April, May, June, September and October.
7½% discount at Laskys/Ace Audio hi-fi stores.
Free entry for two to greyhound tracks.
25% discount on Lingfield Park Racecourse membership rates.

Ordinary 10p or warrants to subscribe for ordinary or 8% Unsec. Loan 1990/92 (no minimum)

Peninsular & Oriental Steam Navigation Co.
P & O Building, Leadenhall Street, London EC3V 4OL

Discounts on ferry rates:
50% on Dover/Boulogne route, 50% on Southampton/Le Havre route, 30% on Liverpool/Belfast route, 30% on Aberdeen/Lerwick route, 30% on Scrabster/Stromness route (the last two routes except July and August). Covers car and passengers but not towed caravans. No limit on number of crossings.

Deferred Stock £1 (200) or 5% Cum. Pfd. Stock £1 (500)

Austin Reed Group
103 Regent Street, London W1A 2AJ

15% discount at company's clothing stores.

Ordinary or 'A' 25p (500)

Sketchley
PO Box 7, Rugby Road, Hinckley, Leicestershire LE10 2NE

25% discount on cleaning and ancillary services.

Ordinary 25p (300) or 4.2% Cum. Pref. £1 (300)

Concession	Qualifying shares (qualifying holding/ registration period)

Trafalgar House Investments
1 Berkeley Street, London W1X 6NN

15% discount on Cunard Line cruises (inc. QE2) and at group hotels.	Ordinary 20p (250)

Trusthouse Forte
PO Box 40, 1 Jermyn Street, London SW1Y 4UH

10% discount on Leisure Gift Cheques which can be used in settlement of the group's hotel and restaurant accounts, overseas holidays or purchases at Lillywhites.	Ordinary 25p or any of the company's 7 quoted debenture or unsecured loan stocks (no minimum)

Note: Prices of the above equities are quoted daily in the *Financial Times*.

15.3   A list of 50 other companies offering concessions

Column (i) shows, where appropriate, the minimum qualifying ordinary shareholding with any relevant qualifying period (in months) in parentheses. Column (ii) shows the form in which the concession is offered. See foot of list for key to other symbols.

Company (area of concession)	Column i	Column ii
Alexanders Holdings (*motor distributors*)	2,000	D
Allied Lyons (*wine and UK hotels*)	—	D&V
Arenson Group (*furniture*)	—	D(15%)
Asprey & Co. (*jewellery, china, etc.*)	375	D(15%)
BL (*new car*)	1,000	D(£100)
BSG International (*motor distributors*)	—	D
Barr & Wallace Arnold (*UK hotels and holidays*)	250 + A	D
Bass (*UK and continental hotels*)	50 + P	D&V
Britannia Arrow (*purchases of unit trusts*)	1,000	D(2%)
Burton Group (*clothing stores*)	—	V
Comfort Hotels (*hotels and restaurants*)	—	D(10%)
*Country Gentlemen's Association** (*mail order*)	100	D
Courts (Furnishers) (*furniture stores*)	100(3m)+A	D(10%)
*Cramphorn** (*garden centres and shops*)	600	D(10%)
Debenhams (*department stores*)	500	D(7½%)
Emess Lighting (*light fittings*)	—	D
Fobel International (*consumer goods*)	—	D
Cecil Gee (*clothing stores*)	500	D(10%)

Company *(area of concession)*	Column i	Column ii
Gieves Group *(clothing)*	600(3M)	D(20%)
Greenall Whitley *(hotels)*	—	D
Greenfields Leisure *(camping and leisure stores)*	100	D(12½%)
Hawley Group *(leisure goods, furniture)*	500	D
House of Fraser *(department stores)*	—	D
Kalon Group *(DIY stores)*	—	D(10%)
Robert Kitchen Taylor *(thermal underwear)*	500	D
Kwik-Fit (Tyres and Exhausts) *(motor parts)*	100	D(10%)
London & Midland Indl. *(home extensions)*	—	D(10%)
London & Northern Group *(double glazing)*	250 + P	D(12½%)
Lonrho *(UK hotels, furnishings)*	100	D
Manders (Holdings) *(DIY stores)*	—	D(10%)
Mellerware *(domestic electrical goods)*	250	D(12½%)
Merrydown Wine *(English wine and cider)*	—	D(20%)
Milletts Leisure Shops *(camping & leisure stores)*	—	D(12½%)
Moss Bros. *(clothing stores)*	250(6m)	D(20%)
Mount Charlotte Investments *(UK hotels)*	1,000	D(10%)
Norfolk Capital Group *(hotels)*	—	D
Pentos *(greenhouses, trailer tents, bookshop)*	500 + Dfd	D
Peters Stores *(clothing and sports stores)*	—	D(15%)
Alfred Preedy & Sons *(stores)*	250	D(10%)
Queens Moat Houses *(UK hotels)*	—	D(£15)
Rank Organisation *(UK and overseas hotels)*	750	D(10%)
Riley Leisure *(snooker and leisure goods)*	—	D
Scottish & Newcastle Breweries *(UK hotels)*	—	D(£15)
Spear & Jackson International *(garden tools)*	—	D(33⅓%)
*****Strikes Restaurants** *(fast food)*	—	D(10%)
Stylo Shoes *(shoe shops)*	—	V
Toye & Co. *(silver and glassware, etc.)*	250	D(15%)
UBM Group *(builders' merchants)*	—	D(10%)
Vaux Breweries *(UK hotels)*	+ P	D(10%)
Whitbread *(wines and spirits)*	—	D

Key to symbols
*	—	Share price not quoted daily in the *Financial Times*.
+ A	—	'A' ordinary shares also qualify.
D	—	Discount rate, where fixed, shown in parentheses; otherwise rate varies.
+ Dfd	—	Deferred shares also qualify.
+ P	—	Preference shares also qualify.
V	—	Voucher.

Section 16

The Trustee Investments Act 1961

16.1 A summary of the Act

The Trustee Investments Act 1961 sets out guidelines for executors and trustees with no specific investment powers who have to administer trust investment funds. Its main purpose is protective and if followed correctly protects the interests of life tenants, ultimate beneficiaries and the trustees as well.

When a trust is initially set up under the Trustee Investments Act the capital resources have to be allocated equally between *narrower-range* and *wider-range* investments as defined in the Act. The investments which may be held in the narrower range are basically of a fixed-interest nature, although Bank of Ireland ordinary stock is the one exception since it has a British Government guarantee. The types of stock which may be held in the wider-range are more broadly based and cover not only fixed interest stocks but also equities (see also section 16.2 for a summary of investments which qualify under the Act). After the initial division of resources between the two ranges, there is no necessity to make compensating transfers to keep the two ranges in equilibrium should the capital performance of one range exceed the other.

When the Act initially applies, it is sometimes necessary to carry out sales of perfectly good stocks because they do not meet the requirements of the Act or, perhaps, because more than 50% of resources is held in ordinary shares. This difficulty can be overcome if the will contains an investment clause conferring upon the trustees the right to retain existing investments. When this circumstance arises, it is possible for the trustees to retain investments in a *special range* although, should any of the securities held in this manner be subsequently sold, any proceeds re-invested must be divided equally between the narrower and wider ranges. However, the attraction of being able to make use of the special range is that it prevents the needless, or premature, disposal of sound investments.

Should the aims of a trust be growth orientated, the fact that narrower-range securities must be of a fixed-interest nature can be an adverse factor. However, the limitation of this feature can be mitigated by purchasing suitable convertible stocks which are regarded as acceptable fixed-interest items. The trustees may not exercise the conversion option and retain the resulting ordinary shares in the narrower range, but this is a minor restriction in practice.

16.2 Qualifying investments

While appointed trustees should always seek professional advice before taking any investment decisions, the following is a summary – with considerable paraphrasing – of the qualifying investments under the Trustee Investments Act 1961, as contained in the First Schedule of Section 1 of the Act.

PART I
NARROWER-RANGE INVESTMENTS NOT REQUIRING ADVICE
1 National Savings Certificates and National Savings Income Bonds.
2 Deposits in the National Savings Bank.

PART II
NARROWER-RANGE INVESTMENTS REQUIRING ADVICE
1 Fixed-interest securities issued by the United Kingdom, Northern Ireland or Isle of Man Governments, and registered in the United Kingdom or the Isle of Man; Treasury bills and Tax Reserve Certificates or variable-interest securities issued by the United Kingdom Government and registered in the United Kingdom.
2 Securities on which interest is guaranteed by the United Kingdom or Northern Ireland Governments.
3 Fixed-interest securities issued in the United Kingdom by public authorities or nationalised undertakings.
4 Fixed-interest or variable-interest securities issued and registered in the United Kingdom by any Commonwealth Government or local authority.
5 Fixed-interest or variable-interest securities issued and registered in the United Kingdom by the International Bank for Reconstruction and Development, the European Investment Bank and the European Coal and Steel Community.

6   Debentures (including bonds, loan stock and notes) registered in the United Kingdom of a company incorporated in the United Kingdom provided the company has an issued share capital of at least £1 million and has paid a dividend on all its issued shares in each of the last five years.
7   Bank of Ireland Stock and 7% Unsecured Loan Stock 1986/91.
8   Debentures of the Agricultural Mortgage Corporation Ltd or the Scottish Agricultural Securities Corporation Ltd.
9   Fixed-interest or variable-interest loans or deposits of local authorities in the United Kingdom.
10   Debentures, guaranteed or preference stock of any statutory water undertakers (Water Act 1945 or corresponding enactment in Northern Ireland) provided the company has paid a dividend of not less than 3½% on its ordinary shares in each of the preceding ten years.
11   Building society deposits.
12   Mortgages on freehold property or leaseholds of 60 years or more in England and Wales or Northern Ireland and loans on heritable security in Scotland.
13   Perpetual rent charges on land in England and Wales or Northern Ireland and fee farm rents, feu duties or ground annuals in Scotland.
14   Certificates of Tax Deposit.

PART III
WIDER-RANGE INVESTMENTS

1   Fully paid-up share capital issued and registered in the United Kingdom by companies incorporated in the United Kingdom which have an issued capital of at least £1 million and have paid a dividend on all issued capital in each of the last five years provided these shares are quoted on a recognised stock exchange.
2   Building society shares.
3   Unit trusts.

PART IV
Part IV contains supplemental – essentially protective – provisions regarding the interpretation and operation of Parts I – III.

Section 17

UK stock market indices

17.1 The Financial Times Industrial Ordinary Index

This is the most widely used barometer of share prices. It is a geometric index of 30 leading industrial shares, calculated and published by the *Financial Times* at hourly intervals from 10 a.m. to the day's close of Stock Exchange business. The index started from a base of 100 in 1935; to the end of September 1986, the all-time peak was 1425.9 (3rd April 1986) and all-time low 49.4 (26th June 1940).

FT Industrial Ordinary Index
Monthly average of index and annual high/low from January 1977
Base = 100 on 1st July 1935

	1977	1978	1979	1980	1981	1982	1983	1984	1985	1986
J	374.7	482.3	474.0	440.6	459.6	543.4	608.4	810.6	977.0	1127.6
F	393.8	457.9	460.2	460.7	487.0	565.6	646.5	814.6	979.3	1220.8
M	418.2	454.9	511.5	440.8	497.7	560.3	659.5	866.4	987.4	1349.0
A	415.1	460.9	537.4	435.4	559.1	563.5	685.6	880.6	969.0	1391.1
M	456.7	476.6	528.5	432.4	557.8	578.7	689.1	869.3	1003.8	1329.6
J	450.5	466.1	489.4	451.2	545.0	569.9	716.5	824.5	980.4	1332.1
J	443.1	472.2	468.3	488.5	528.1	559.6	698.0	787.6	935.2	1309.6
A	478.6	508.8	467.2	484.9	554.4	561.1	724.4	835.8	973.6	1262.1
S	522.7	515.9	468.4	491.7	525.0	580.6	704.4	859.3	1002.8	
O	511.9	497.5	465.4	483.8	474.4	601.9	693.5	865.1	1034.2	
N	480.4	476.9	415.9	493.4	511.0	618.7	724.8	912.7	1099.3	
D	481.6	482.4	419.8	470.1	522.8	592.8	759.5	929.6	1113.7	
H*	549.2	535.5	558.6	515.9	597.3	637.4	776.2	952.3	1146.9	
L*	357.6	433.6	406.3	406.9	446.0	518.1	598.4	755.3	911.0	

* Actual high/low for year.

Constituents of the FT Industrial Ordinary Index *(may be changed from time to time)*

Allied Lyons
ASDA-MFI Group
BICC
BOC Group
BTR
Beecham Group
Blue Circle Industries
Boots
British Petroleum
British Telecom
Cadbury Schweppes
Courtaulds
General Electric Company
Glaxo Holdings
Grand Metropolitan

Guest Keen & Nettlefolds
Guinness
Hanson Trust
Hawker Siddeley
Imperial Chemical Industries
Lucas Industries
Marks & Spencer
National Westminster Bank
P&O Steam
Plessey
Royal Insurance
Tate & Lyle
Thorn EMI
Trusthouse Forte
Vickers

17.2 The Financial Times Actuaries Share Indices

This is a detailed series of indices, earnings and yield averages, covering a wide range of equity groups, sub-sections and fixed-interest securities, produced and published daily by the *Financial Times,* in co-operation with the Institution of Actuaries and the Faculty of Actuaries. The indices are base weighted and so measure the change in value of a hypothetical portfolio of shares, where the holdings are in proportion to the market capitalisation of the companies. The most widely used index in the series is the All-Share Index. This covers 750 shares, including a selection from the financial sector. It is therefore a better indicator of longer term trends in share prices than the *Financial Times* Industrial Ordinary Index, which is confined at any one time to just 30 mostly industrial market leaders.

FT – Actuaries All-Share Index
Index numbers and average gross dividend yield at quarterly intervals from
1st January 1977.
Base = 100 on 1st April 1962

	1st January Index	Yield	1st April Index	Yield	1st July Index	Yield	1st October Index	Yield
1977	151.9	6.42	173.4	5.81	189.3	5.57	226.0	4.86
1978	214.5	5.28	203.8	5.70	209.9	5.70	227.1	5.48
1979	220.2	5.79	266.6	4.93	248.3	5.32	254.0	5.99
1980	229.8	6.87	243.7	6.82	267.0	6.46	292.4	6.08
1981	292.0	6.10	311.4	5.74	321.8	5.63	279.0	6.56
1982	313.1	5.89	327.8	5.79	320.8	6.13	360.5	5.53
1983	382.2	5.26	439.3	4.68	453.8	4.60	445.3	4.80
1984	470.5	4.62	522.9	4.39	490.5	4.87	531.3	4.72
1985	592.9	4.42	616.6	4.47	600.5	4.79	629.3	4.61
1986	682.9	4.33	818.2	3.75	820.3	3.84		

All-time high (to end September 1986) : 832.4 (3rd April 1986)
All-time low (to end September 1986) : 61.9 (13th December 1974)

17.3 The Financial Times/Stock Exchange 100 Index

The Financial Times/Stock Exchange 100 Index is a comparatively new measure of the market, having started from a
base of 1,000 on 3rd January 1984. It is an unweighted index of
the 100 largest UK companies (by market capitalisation) quoted
on The Stock Exchange. Inevitably, these change from time to
time, and the constituents are reviewed quarterly. The unique
feature of the index is that it is recalculated on a minute-by-
minute basis, thus giving a virtually constant picture of the
overall trend in share prices. The index was created to support a
futures contract based upon the UK equity market.

FTSE 100 Index
Index numbers at quarterly intervals from 1st January 1984.
Base = 100 on 3rd January 1984

	1st January	1st April	1st July	1st October
1984	1000.0 (3rd)	1108.1	1047.6	1127.7
1985	1232.2	1278.3	1246.8	1296.0
1986	1412.6	1684.0	1660.8	

All-time high (to end September 1986) : 1717.6 (3rd April 1986)
All-time low (to end September 1986) : 986.9 (23rd July 1984)

Section 18

Major UK economic indicators

18.1 Balance of payments (current account)

Often referred to as the 'trade figures', the balance of payments is a monthly statement of the United Kingdom's current account trade position with other countries. It encompasses visible trade, i.e. in merchandise of all types, and invisible trade, i.e. in services where no goods are involved. The latter is the balance of profits earned by such industries as banking, insurance, tourism and shipping, less expenditure, mainly by Government, e.g. Foreign Office, on overseas services. Visible trade is broken down into import and export figures and the balance is shown as a deficit or surplus.

Example

A typical set of monthly figures might be presented as follows:

	£ million
Exports	3,050
Imports	3,120
Visible balance	− 70
Invisible balance	+ 120
Current account balance	+ 50

The ripples of unanticipated changes in the balance of payments can spread much more widely, with potential impact on currency exchange rates and interest rates and all the 'knock-on' effects this implies. Thus, the release of these trade figures can have an immediate impact on stock market trends if they differ widely from general expectations.

18.2 Money supply

Broadly speaking, this may be defined as the amount of money in the economy at a given time. Money supply is the central pillar of monetarism, a branch of economic theory which claims that the sharp increase in the rate of inflation in the mid 1970s was the result of the money supply being allowed to grow more rapidly than the economy's output. In recent years there has been a transition to monetarist-based economic policies and the monthly money supply figures have assumed greater significance.

Money supply growth means that cash and deposits in the banking system are rising and, if the rate of growth looks excessive, controls may be introduced to reduce their inflationary potential. These controls can take various forms, such as increased interest rates and direct controls over bank lending. There are five measurements of money supply, as follows:

 i *M0*, a wide measure, consisting of notes and coins in circulation with the public, plus Banks' till money and Banks' operational balances with the Bank of England.
 ii *M1*, the narrow version, consisting of notes and coins in circulation with the public plus sterling sight deposits held by the private sector only.
iii *M2*, comprising notes and coins in circulation with the public, non-interest-bearing private sector sterling sight deposits and private sector retail deposits.
iv *Sterling M3*, comprising notes and coins in circulation with the public, together with all sterling deposits (including certificates of deposit) held by UK residents in the private sector.
 v *M3*, which is Sterling M3, as in (iv) above, plus all deposits held by UK residents in other currencies.

In all definitions deposits are confined to those with institutions included in the UK monetary sector less 60% of the net value of sterling transit items.

18.3 Public sector borrowing requirement (PSBR)

For the purpose of financial transactions, the public sector encompasses central government, local authorities and public corporations. The PSBR indicates the extent to which the expenditure of the public sector exceeds, or is expected to exceed, its receipts, and which must therefore be financed by borrowings from other sources. This deficit is financed in three main ways: by creation of debt to the public outside the banking system, for example, the issue of gilt-edged and local authority stocks via The Stock Exchange and National Savings; by borrowing from the banking system; and by certain external (overseas) transactions. Of these, the issue of gilt-edged securities finances by far the greater part of the borrowing requirement.

In effect, the borrowing accumulated over the years by the public sector (the National Debt) represents an 'overdraft' of massive proportions. Ideally, therefore, public sector expenditure would balance with its receipts, and it has been forcefully argued that, if a Government deliberately increases its PSBR to promote a higher level of economic activity, it should at least reduce the PSBR, or even accumulate surpluses, in economically more buoyant times. This, it is suggested, would reduce the inherent volatility of economic activity and keep the National Debt within reasonable bounds.

If the PSBR is rising faster than increases in the nation's wealth then, in effect, the Government will have to print money to pay for the excess, or raise taxes which it is seldom willing to do. This is one of the main sources of inflation and hence the constant cry to cut public expenditure. The difficulty of running an ideal PSBR policy of rough long term balance, as described above, lies in the lack of political will to withdraw, during periods of buoyancy, money stimulants given by Governments in times of recession. Too often therefore, Governments find themselves in the position of acting pro-cyclically: trying to cut the PSBR in recessions and allowing it to rise when economic recovery has been achieved. The former is unlikely to succeed and the latter doomed to inflation. Thus the PSBR figures can have an important bearing on trends in the gilt-edged and equity markets.

18.4 Retail Price Index (RPI)

Sometimes referred to as 'the cost of living' index, this is a monthly index of prices paid by consumers for the goods and services between which their expenditure is typically divided, with a heavier weighting towards areas of major expenditure, such as housing and food. Interpretation of the RPI can be difficult as any one month's figures can be distorted by special factors. Month-on-month figures, therefore, must be treated with care; the year-on-year figures provide a fairer guide to reality.

Retail Price Index – 1
(Annually from January 1970)

Date January	Index no.	Year-on-year increase †
1970	70.6*	
1971	76.6*	8.5%
1972	82.9*	8.2%
1973	89.3*	7.7%
1974	100.0	12.0%
1975	119.9	19.9%
1976	147.9	23.3%
1977	172.4	16.5%
1978	189.5	9.9%
1979	207.2	9.3%
1980	245.3	18.4%
1981	277.3	13.0%
1982	310.6	12.0%
1983	325.9	4.9%
1984	342.6	5.1%
1985	359.8	5.0%
1986	379.7	5.5%

† i.e. the annual rate of UK price inflation for the previous year.
* the RPI currently published by the Central Statistical Office commenced from a base of 100.0 in January 1974. The index numbers shown for January 1970–73 have been converted to this base from the previous scale which has a base of 100.0 in January 1962 (52.1 on the January 1974 base).

The introduction of indexation of capital gains for tax purposes (see section S2) with effect from 6th April 1982 has brought with it the need to refer to the RPI for the relevant months of acquisition and disposal of the shareholding or other asset concerned. To assist readers in this respect the following table contains a listing of the RPI from 1982 onwards on a monthly basis, up to the last possible date prior to the publication of this book. The RPI (for the preceding month) is released normally on the third Friday of each month.

Retail Price Index – 2
(Monthly from January 1982)

	Jan	Feb	Mar	Apr	May	Jun	July	Aug	Sept	Oct	Nov	Dec
1982	310.6	310.7	313.4	319.7	322.0	322.9	323.0	323.1	322.9	324.5	326.1	325.5
1983	325.9	327.3	327.9	332.5	333.9	334.7	336.5	338.0	339.5	340.7	341.9	342.8
1984	342.6	344.0	345.1	349.7	351.0	351.9	351.5	354.8	355.5	357.7	358.8	358.5
1985	359.8	362.7	366.1	373.9	375.6	376.4	375.7	376.7	376.5	377.1	378.4	378.9
1986	379.7	381.1	381.6	385.3	386.0	385.8	384.7					

Section 19

Stock Exchange statistics

19.1 Stock Exchange turnover

Stock Exchange annual turnover
The aggregate of purchases and sales from 1976

	Fixed interest		Equity		Total	
	No. of bargains	Value (Av. per bargain)	No. of bargains	Value (Av. per bargain)	No. of bargains	Value (Av. per bargain)
1976	1,299,439	£92,270m (£71,008)	3,566,727	£14,163m (£3,970)	4,866,166	£106,433m (£21,872)
1977	1,650,105	£153,166m (£92,822)	4,434,522	£20,168m (£4,548)	6,084,627	£173,334m (£28,487)
1978	1,359,866	£119,554m (£87,916)	4,129,963	£19,215m (£4,652)	5,489,829	£138,769m (£25,277)
1979	1,344,131	£144,831m (£107,750)	4,111,774	£24,106m (£5,863)	5,455,905	£168,937m (£30,964)
1980	1,477,277	£165,489m (£112,023)	4,230,737	£30,801m (£7,280)	5,708,014	£196,290m (£34,388)
1981	1,343,827	£158,280m (£117,783)	3,944,495	£32,387m (£8,211)	5,288,322	£190,667m (£36,054)
1982	1,504,693	£222,330m (£147,758)	3,883,112	£37,414m (£9,635)	5,387,805	£259,744m (£48,210)
1983	1,279,210	£231,456m (£180,937)	4,726,273	£56,131m (£11,876)	6,005,483	£287,587m (£47,887)
1984	1,202,429	£291,557m (£242,473)	4,848,671	£73,119m (£15,080)	6,051,100	£364,676m (£60,266)
1985	1,141,667	£284,920m (£249,564)	5,567,798	£105,554m (£18,957)	6,709,465	£390,474m (£58,197)

Source: *The Stock Exchange Fact Book*

19.2 Listed securities statistics

Stock Exchange listed securities
Market values and number of securities from 1976

| End March | Public sector & Eurobonds | | UK companies* | | Overseas companies | | All securities |
	Govt stocks* Mkt value £m (No. secs)	Other Mkt value £m (No. secs)	Fixed interest Mkt value £m (No. secs)	Equities Mkt value £m (No. secs)	Fixed interest Mkt value £m (No. secs)	Equities Mkt value £m (No. secs)	Mkt value £m (No. secs)
1976	27,777 *152*	5,775 *1,378*	4,753 *3,837*	44,819 *2,887*	414 *105*	190,317 *384*	273,855 *8,743*
1977	38,231 *150*	6,754 *1,371*	5,154 *3,697*	48,975 *2,691*	422 *91*	193,692 *381*	293,228 *8,381*
1978	49,952 *162*	8,952 *1,408*	5,686 *3,539*	58,181 *2,560*	435 *86*	179,380 *388*	302,586 *8,143*
1979	57,945 *176*	9,118 *1,432*	5,844 *3,400*	78,390 *2,440*	502 *91*	176,532 *383*	328,331 *7,922*
1980	60,780 *193*	8,744 *1,496*	4,447 *3,275*	71,316 *2,332*	728 *87*	134,312 *391*	280,327 *7,774*
1981	78,769 *194*	12,670 *1,309*	5,350 *3,101*	92,683 *2,234*	710 *86*	185,748 *392*	375,930 *7,316*
1982	83,544 *180*	22,506 *1,427*	6,036 *2,986*	104,640 *2,132*	729 *83*	238,550 *396*	456,005 *7,204*
1983	101,733 *195*	38,340 *1,565*	8,362 *2,858*	132,905 *2,016*	1,027 *81*	406,125 *411*	688,492 *7,126*
1984	116,074 *204*	45,039 *1,620*	9,023 *2,669*	173,272 *1,982*	1,806 *90*	483,042 *405*	828,256 *6,970*
1985	123,497 *214*	76,749 *1,617*	9,116 *2,521*	217,422 *1,908*	3,525 *149*	675,690 *462*	1,105,999 *6,871*
1986	146,815 *213*	84,804 *1,636*	10,656 *2,377*	295,083 *1,904*	3,934 *142*	703,614 *440*	1,244,906 *6,712*

* Including Irish securities from 1976.　　**Source:** *The Stock Exchange Fact Book*

19.3 New issues and redemptions

Government issues and redemptions and company issues less redemptions
Stock Exchange listed securities issued by UK borrowers/companies only from 1976

	Government securities		Local authorities and public corporations* £m	Company securities*				
	Cash issues £m	Cash redemptions £m		Convertible loan capital £m	Other loan capital £m	Preference shares £m	Ordinary shares £m	Total £m
1976	8,332	2,405	108	8	− 12	31	1,054	1,081
1977	12,647	2,643	239	− 5	− 70	16	789	730
1978	7,323	2,425	48	− 21	− 92	22	925	834
1979	14,114	3,589	−170	23	−105	54	960	932
1980	14,851	3,606	−166	178	−228	29	953	932
1981	12,826	5,338	−157	194	−265	68	1,835	1,832
1982	10,574	4,666	−174	8	187	8	964	1,167
1983	14,538	6,355	− 66	47	518	59	2,188	2,812
1984	13,956	5,003	−258	101	180	42	1,398	1,721
1985	15,192	5,960	−566	320	166	414	4,210	5,110

*These estimates relate to new money raised by all types of new issues, including new listings and rights issues, less redemptions.
Source: *Central Statistical Office – 'Financial Statistics'*

19.4   The 40 largest UK companies

The 40 largest UK companies
By market valuation as at 31st March 1986

		Market value £ million				Market value £ million
1	British Telecommunications	15,600		21	Unilever PLC	2,450
2	British Petroleum	10,212		22	Distillers	2,433
3	Shell Transport & Trading	8,618		23	Lloyds Bank	2,344
4	Glaxo Holdings	7,402		24	Rio Tinto Zinc Corpn	2,229
5	Imperial Chemical Industries	6,196		25	Allied Lyons	2,213
6	BAT Industries	5,971		26	Royal Insurance	2,061
7	Marks & Spencer	5,582		27	Sears	2,031
8	BTR	5,250		28	Boots	1,920
9	General Electric Co.	5,013		29	Wellcome	1,871
10	Barclays	3,854		30	Burton Group	1,797
11	Cable & Wireless	3,504		31	ASDA-MFI Group	1,650
12	Grand Metropolitan	3,459		32	General Accident	1,630
13	Hanson Trust	3,404		33	Land Securities	1,586
14	National Westminster Bank	3,302		34	BOC Group	1,556
15	J. Sainsbury	2,775		35	Tarmac	1,535
16	Prudential Corpn	2,733		36	Plessey	1,525
17	Beecham Group	2,713		37	Dee Corporation	1,523
18	Bass	2,697		38	Trusthouse Forte	1,522
19	Imperial Group	2,586		39	Tesco	1,473
20	Great Universal Stores	2,460		40	British Aerospace	1,425

Source: *Stock Exchange Companies*

Section 20

Investing overseas

20.1 The case for investing overseas

Statistics show that most investors worldwide tend to concentrate their capital in their domestic investment markets. This is not really surprising, given the array of investment opportunities available to the individual and the difficulties that can be encountered in obtaining information about overseas investments, while there is an understandable psychological tendency to keep one's capital near to home. UK investors are no exception to this rule although, on top of the foregoing, a further disincentive to investment abroad by UK citizens was the existence for more than 40 years of exchange control regulations. Now that these controls have been removed the world has again become the UK investor's oyster; we are now free to invest as much as we like, where we like, in what we like – be it in securities, property, gold or other commodities or just foreign currency.

So what is the significance of this new-found freedom for the private investor and what are the practical aspects of investing abroad? The most obvious merit of being able to invest overseas without restriction is that it gives the UK investor more flexibility to diversify or switch the geographical base of his invested capital into countries which may at any time seem to offer better investment potential than the United Kingdom, or simply to spread his risks – a policy with considerable merit in this era of international economic and political instability. Furthermore, opportunities – or at least a greater choice – of investment in areas not readily or directly available in the United Kingdom often exist in overseas markets, examples of this being certain natural resources, areas of high technology and private health care.

As within the UK market, the choice overseas lies essentially between bonds – fixed-interest securities – and equities, although, in recent years, the greater part of what foreign portfolio investment there has been by UK private investors has been concentrated on the latter category. This can be attributed to two main factors. Firstly, the existence of the investment currency premium prior to October 1979 not only reduced the yield on foreign bonds to a UK investor but added a further dimension of risk (due to the premium's fluctuations), over and above that of exchange rate and local market price movements, to a type of investment which should be comparatively risk free. Secondly, yields in the UK fixed-interest market have for a long time compared favourably with those available abroad and, with the gilt-edged sector in particular offering capital gains tax advantages and a high degree of liquidity, UK investors seeking fixed-interest investments have, for most purposes, generally tended to look no further afield than the UK market. This situation seems unlikely to change dramatically in the near future at least and, despite the abolition of exchange controls, the indications are that the UK gilt-edged market will maintain its position as the UK investor's primary choice for fixed-interest capital investments.

On the other hand, and for the reasons set out earlier, diversification into foreign equity markets, especially for capital growth orientated portfolios, can now be more objectively considered as an alternative to concentrating solely on UK shares. In this connection, the London market is unique in that facilities exist for dealing in, or obtaining information about, almost any share listed on an overseas stock exchange, provided a ready domestic market exists. This apart, more foreign equities (over 400) have an 'official' listing in London than on any other stock exchange. Principal among these are about 200 US equities, 100 South Africans – mostly gold-mining companies – with the remainder registered in over 30 other countries.

For most private investors, particularly those with comparatively limited resources, unit trusts or investment trusts represent the most convenient and cheapest method of investing abroad, since dealing in 'small parcels' of individual foreign securities can often be comparatively expensive and undesirable from a marketability point of view. Through the medium of unit trusts or investment trusts, a wide market coverage, under professional management, can be encompassed within the one investment, while investors usually receive half-yearly reports on the progress of the underlying fund. A wide range of UK-based (sterling-denominated) funds is available, covering most major overseas markets either individually or collectively. However, there is also a wide choice of 'offshore' (see section 11.6) or foreign based investment funds, many of which are listed in leading UK financial journals, such as the *Financial Times,* thus enabling the UK investor to monitor their performance fairly easily.

Nevertheless, the private investor with adequate funds at his disposal should not be discouraged from investing directly in overseas stocks and shares, although there is a wide divergence of opinion as to just how much is 'adequate'. This will depend to a large extent on the market and type of security under consideration, dealing costs and, of course, the individual investor's overall capital position and own views or preferences. In short, there can be no firm rules on the subject but, as indicated earlier, it is generally advisable to avoid small purchases and in this connection section 21, which describes the principal overseas equity markets, includes the suggested minimum unit of investment figures with comments as appropriate.

20.2 Foreign currency bonds

Foreign bonds are most likely to attract the UK investor seeking a safe – *vis-à-vis* equity – investment in a currency which is expected to appreciate in value against the pound, thus enhancing the value of the interest receivable and the capital invested when the bond is sold or redeemed and the proceeds converted back into sterling – although, of course, this is a two-way risk. From an investor's point of view, it would be convenient if international secondary markets in Government bonds – their implied security would make these most investors' ideal choice – had evolved some form of standardisation in terms of accessibility and dealing procedures. However, the fact is that the UK gilt-edged market is without comparison overseas, reflecting largely the British Government's unique, centralised, method of fund raising. Foreign governments and public authorities tend to borrow on a more fragmented basis, in many cases through 'over-the-counter' bond issues, with no single centralised secondary market. In practical investment terms, this means that most foreign Government bond markets are rather inaccessible to the UK investor, the major exception being US Treasury issues, although a drawback here is that individual transactions in sums of less than about $50,000 are regarded as 'small', with a consequent disadvantage in price and marketability. Most overseas stock markets do have a corporate bond sector, broadly comparable with UK company debenture and loan stocks, but the investor seeking a foreign currency bond investment will usually be advised to consider the 'Eurobond' market (see below).

20.3 Eurobonds

The Eurobond market provides a source of fixed-term overseas borrowings, usually underwritten by a syndicate of international financial organisations, for major companies, public agencies and Governments. Secondary market trading is transacted by telephone between members of the Association of International Bond Dealers (AIBD), although many bonds are quoted on stock exchanges around the world (over 600 are officially listed in London). The Eurobond market is probably the most practical investment area for UK residents seeking a fixed-term bond investment in a foreign currency which they expect to appreciate in value against the pound, but there are a number of important points or features that interested investors should bear in mind:

i   A wide range of short- and long-maturity bonds is available denominated in various currencies, including 'hard' currencies such as the Swiss franc, Japanese yen and German Deutschmark, although, not surprisingly, US dollar issues account for a relatively high proportion of the market. It is generally advisable to concentrate on larger issues by well-known international organisations or companies.

ii The minimum practical investment in a single bond is $10,000 or its equivalent in other currencies. Quotations for smaller 'parcels' may be difficult to obtain and can be unfavourable.

iii   Bonds are generally traded in multiples of 1,000 units nominal of the underlying currency, e.g. in multiples of $1,000, subject to the minimum mentioned in (ii) above.

iv   Interest is payable gross, i.e. without deduction of any taxes, but it is, of course, fully assessable in the normal way to UK income tax, where the investor is a UK taxpayer ordinarily.

v   Only one interest payment is made per annum. This means that careful attention should be paid to the accrued interest position; as a general rule, most private investors attracted by this market will want to avoid bonds incorporating a large amount of accrued interest.

vi   Apart from straight fixed-coupon bonds, variations include floating-rate bonds and corporate bonds which have warrants or conversion rights attached, entitling holders to subscribe for, or convert into, the issuing company's equity on predetermined terms.

vii   Eurobonds are issued in bearer form.

viii   A number of 'offshore' investment funds specialising in Eurobonds are available and these, offering professional management and potentially better liquidity, may be seen as a more attractive proposition than individual bond holdings for many private investors and certainly for those with a smaller sum at their disposal than that mentioned in (ii) above.

20.4 Gold

Throughout history, gold has stood as the ultimate symbol and measurement of wealth, the accepted standard by all trading nations. This, together with its universal marketability, has often made it an attractive haven for investment funds during long periods of international political or economic uncertainty, when the risks of holding currency, or currency denominated assets, may appear high. There are two principal ways in which the investor can take an interest in gold:

i   By purchasing shares in a gold-mining company (or a unit fund specialising in gold shares). These are, of course, subject to the usual supply and demand influences discussed in section 7.2, the demand – or lack of it – usually reflecting investor expectation of future gold price levels. The shares of all companies whose profits – and thus dividends – are dependent on commodity prices, which in turn are dictated by the same supply and demand rules, carry an extra degree of risk. However, in return for the above-average risk, shareholders in gold-mining companies can normally anticipate above-average yields in particularly profitable years and these may well result in higher prices for the shares.

ii   By purchasing gold coins. This is the most practical way of physically possessing gold other than through jewellery where a more substantial premium over the value of the gold content has to be paid for the craftsmanship involved. The coin generally recommended is the *Krugerrand,* which is a South African coin containing one ounce of 24 carat gold. The price of the one ounce Krugerrand, which, of all gold coins, normally trades at the smallest premium to the value of its gold content, moves broadly in line with the bullion price and is therefore a purer form of investment in gold than gold-mining shares, where other considerations may influence market prices; however, it must be remembered that gold coins produce no dividends. Purchases of Krugerrands attract VAT if made through a UK mainland dealer or if delivery to the buyer is completed. This can be avoided if, for example, the coins are bought through, and stored by (for a modest charge), a Channel Islands-based dealer.

The tax treatment of gains realised on a disposal of Krugerrands or other gold coins will depend on the circumstances of each transaction. As a general rule, the gain is treated as income and taxed as such but, in the case of 'isolated' or long-term transactions, the Inland Revenue may accept that the coins were held as assets for capital gain and charge to tax accordingly; if such a claim is ultimately to be made, it is recommended that investors enter the purchase in the section of their income tax return which records acquisitions of chargeable assets. Investors in doubt as to their tax position should consult their usual tax adviser.

Notes:
i   A guide to the market prices of the principal *investment* gold coins appears in the *Financial Times.*
ii   See following page for a summary of the price of gold at annual intervals from 1st January 1970.

Gold
Market price at annual intervals from 1st January 1970

Date	Price US$ per ounce	Date	Price US$ per ounce
1st January 1970	35.2	1st January 1978	165.1
,, 1971	37.3	,, 1979	226.4
,, 1972	43.6	,, 1980	526.5
,, 1973	64.9	,, 1981	589.5
,, 1974	111.7	,, 1982	400.0
,, 1975	186.0	,, 1983	448.0
,, 1976	140.5	,, 1984	382.0
,, 1977	134.6	,, 1985	309.0
		,, 1986	327.2

Notes:

i   A listing of the *Rand Daily Mail Gold Index* at quarterly intervals from 1st January 1975 will be found in section 22.5.

ii The above prices can be converted to sterling by using the US dollar:sterling exchange rates given in section 22.2.

Section 21
Overseas equity markets

The purpose of this section is to outline briefly the features and characteristics of the major overseas equity markets, particularly from a UK investor's point of view, and to suggest how an interest in the various markets might best be taken. The suggested minimum direct investments typically relate to portfolios of £50,000 and over; for smaller portfolios unit trusts can be recommended. A corresponding list of overseas equity indices follows in section 22. The 'domestic equity market' statistics relate only to equities quoted on the stock exchanges named; they do not necessarily represent the full extent of a country's equity market, since many have regional stock exchanges as well. 'London listed' refers to the number of shares with an official listing on the London Stock Exchange.

For the record, comparable statistics for the UK equity market are as under:

	Companies listed (end 1985)	Market value (end 1985) £bn	Turnover (1985) £bn
UK	2,116	244.7	52.8

Note: The turnover is half that shown in section 19.1, to comply with the method of recording turnover in overseas markets.

21.1 North America

Domestic equity markets:

	Companies listed (end 1985)	Market value (end 1985) £bn	Turnover (1985) £bn	London listed (March 1986)
USA (New York SE)	1,487	1,302.2	671.3	192
Canada (Toronto SE)	912	108.9	21.8	28

Characteristics: The New York Stock Exchange is easily the world's largest, with an equity market about three times the size (by value) of its nearest rival – Tokyo – and six times as large as London. Both the NYSE and the Toronto SE attract around 80% of their country's equity trading, the remainder being accounted for by regional exchanges and 'over-the-counter' markets, the latter, incidentally, including also the bulk of trading in both countries' Government bonds. Share prices of leading companies on both markets – particularly New York – tend to be 'heavier' than in the United Kingdom, with the equivalent of £10-£30 being the typical range, but this should not be regarded as a disincentive by UK investors, who are generally more used to lower London prices. Nevertheless, for marketability reasons, it is normally advisable to deal in a minimum of 100 shares.

The United States has traditionally been seen as a major alternative investment area to the United Kingdom and the case for participation in its economy through equity representation in private UK portfolios placing an emphasis on capital appreciation has been strengthened by the removal of exchange control legislation. Canada, with its important natural resources, can often merit consideration as a complementary area. For larger portfolios a selection of individual US/Canadian equities can usually be recommended; for sums of less than £4,000 earmarked for these markets, unit trusts or investment trusts will be more suitable.

A wide range of broadly based US or North American (including Canada) unit trusts is available to the UK investor, although a number of specialised funds – for example concentrating on companies involved in high technology, smaller companies or even 'recovery situations' – have appeared in recent years. There are few – if any – unit trusts exclusively devoted to the Canadian market; investors seeking a purely Canadian interest would need to consider a fund domiciled in Canada.

Suggested minimum direct investment:

American equities £3,000   Subject preferably to a minimum of 100
Canadian equities £3,000   shares. The shares should be held in a
recognised marking name, unless bearer
shares.

21.2 The Far East

Domestic equity markets:

	Companies listed (end 1985)	Market value (end 1985) £bn	Turnover (1985) £bn	London listed (March 1986)
Japan *(Tokyo SE)*	1,476	648.7	271.5	8
Hong Kong *(All exchanges)*	247	40.8	Not available	2
Malaysia *(Singapore SE)*	122	27.9	2.5	17

Characteristics: Second only in size to the United States, more than twice as large as London by total value, the Japanese equity market, supported by an expanding economy and a strong currency, proved one of the major growth areas of the last decade. However, direct investment in Japanese equities is mainly for specialists and the UK investor wishing to take an interest in this market will normally be advised to do so through the medium of units trusts.

Hong Kong is recognised as one of the most volatile of the world's established equity markets, as the index history in section 22.3 illustrates and, unlike London or New York, local private investors and syndicates account for the bulk of trading activity; this is also true of the Singapore market. The Hong Kong market is dominated by the shares of the long-established trading houses, banks, property and shipping companies. The volatility of this market tends to attract a good deal of speculative activity and long-term portfolio representation is, for most UK investors, best obtained through the major trading houses and banks.

The Singapore market is closely linked to the Kuala Lumpur market, with many shares listed on both, and is best known externally for its commodity shares – mainly rubber, palm oil, plantations and tin. This also tends to be a volatile market, especially the plantations sector, where even the weather can be a major influence, owing to its potential effect on crop levels and thus company earnings and dividends.

The Far East is now well covered by the UK unit trust industry, the choice lying essentially between funds wholly invested in Japan or funds covering the Far East as a general investment area, where the proportions held in any one country will vary in accordance with the managers' assessment of individual market prospects.

Suggested minimum direct investment:

Japanese equities	£2,000	Must be held in Japan. Normally subject to a minimum of 1,000 shares. Unit trusts are recommended.
Hong Kong equities	£2,000	Market leaders only recommended.
Malaysian equities	£2,000	

21.3 Australia

Domestic equity markets:

	Companies listed (end 1985)	Market value (end 1985) £bn	Turnover (1985) £bn	London listed (March 1986)
All exchanges	1,069	41.6	22.4	12

Characteristics: The Australian market can be divided into two main sectors: the commercial/industrial markets and the more volatile oil/mining markets. The latter contain scores of small exploration companies and, in recent years in particular, have produced some of the most spectacular share price rises – and falls – seen anywhere on the world's stock markets. Inevitably, therefore, and particularly during periods of buoyancy, this market tends to attract a good deal of speculative activity.

However, the risks associated with the smaller exploration issues are normally considered too high for the average investor and those wishing to participate in the undoubted investment potential inherent in Australia's immense natural resources are generally advised to restrict their choice to the larger and well-established mining groups.

A ready market in most Australian shares exists in London, while unit trust representation is available, some providing a balance of investments between the main commercial and industrial areas as well as natural resources, while others concentrate exclusively on the latter.

Suggested minimum direct investment:

Commercial/industrial
equities   £2,000
Oil/mining equities:
leaders   £2,000
Small exploration issues   £500

Must be regarded as high-risk capital. Dealing in small amounts can be comparatively expensive, while it is frequently possible to deal only in multiples of 100 or even 1,000 shares, especially in the case of low-priced issues.

21.4 South Africa

Domestic equity market:

	Companies listed (end 1985)	Market value (end 1985) £bn	Turnover (1985) £bn	London listed (March 1986)
Johannesburg SE	501	37.2	1.7	94

Characteristics: As with Australia, the South African stock market is divided into two distinct sectors, in this case the domestic commercial/industrial market and the world's principal gold-mining companies. Important markets in South African 'golds' exist in London and New York, while leading industrials are generally readily marketable in London, even though the country's political sensitivities have in recent years acted as a disincentive to large-scale investment in South Africa by foreign residents. However, with few alternatives elsewhere, South

African golds remain the prime area for consideration by those investors seeking to introduce an interest in gold mining to their portfolios. Further comments on gold will be found in section 20.4.

A significant exposure to South African industrials is difficult to find among unit trusts, although many general funds contain a small proportion of gold-mining shares and a number of funds specialising in golds alone are available – these merit consideration by the smaller or more cautious investor with limited resources who nevertheless wishes to take an interest in this market.

Suggested minimum direct investment:
Commercial/industrial
equities   £2,000
Gold-mining equities   £1,000   Above-average risk/reward ratio.

21.5 Continental Europe

Domestic equity markets:

	Companies listed (end 1985)	Market value (end 1985) £bn	Turnover (1985) £bn	London listed (March 1986)
Germany (All exchanges)	451	123.8	68.8	7
France (Paris SE)	489	58.5	14.5	4
Switzerland (Zürich SE)	131	76.2	Not available	1
Netherlands (Amsterdam SE)	232	41.2	14.2	15

Characteristics: Until the early 1980s, trends in the major Continental European equity markets were generally less volatile than those seen in London, as the index listings in section 22 illustrate. This was in part due to underlying economic considerations (for instance, much lower inflation rates) and in part to the *modus operandi* of the individual markets, including the dominant position often held by Continental banks and financial organisations in both the stock market and, as shareholders themselves, in industry. Thus, European equities did not attract a great deal of attention from UK investors. However, most Continental European markets have 'woken up' in recent years with a dramatic burst of strength and selected shares from these markets can merit consideration for inclusion in larger portfolios, especially as vehicles for providing an interest in the underlying domestic currency.

There is a ready market in London in most leading German and French shares, although dealing in Swiss equities can be rather more difficult. Trading in Dutch shares is mainly limited to the handful of so-called 'internationals' which also have a London quotation. Unit trust coverage of Continental Europe is confined mostly to the area as a whole, with the proportions invested in any one country varying with the manager's assessment of individual market prospects. However, one or two trusts wholly invested in Germany appeared in 1985.

Suggested minimum direct investment:

German equities	£2,000	
French equities	£2,000	Market leaders only recommended.
Swiss equities	£2,000	
Dutch equities	£2,000	

Section 22

Overseas equity market indices

The index numbers listed in sections 22.2 – 22.6 (arranged in an order corresponding to section 21) are the actual index numbers that apply on the dates shown, i.e. at three-monthly intervals commencing 1st January 1975, with the underlying currency's exchange rate against sterling shown only as at 1st January each year. For comparison purposes, corresponding listings of the UK's Financial Times Industrial Ordinary Index will be found in section 22.7.

22.1 General comments

This section has been included both for general reference purposes and for the statistically minded investor armed with a home computer or a sheet of graph paper and an interest in the trends in recent years of the major overseas equity markets covered in section 21, as measured by their principal indices.

The index listings do, however, illustrate almost at a glance certain events witnessed in the international investment arena during the last decade or so. Some of the more pronounced examples are the solid growth of the Japanese market; the volatility of Hong Kong; the effect of the girations in the price of gold on South African gold-mining shares; the comparatively dull nature of the Continental European markets until recent years and what was perhaps the major event from a UK investor's point of view – the decline of sterling against many of the world's leading currencies, especially the dollar, during the mid 1970s, its

133

temporary recovery as it gained petro-currency status in the late 1970s/early 1980s and its renewed downward slide from 1982 onwards.

The inclusion of the currency exchange rates as at 1st January each year does facilitate a broad comparison of the performance of the various markets in sterling terms, albeit on a limited and random basis from one 1st January to another, and section 22.8 shows the calculations necessary to convert an index to a sterling basis.

What does emerge from these statistics, and remains as true today as ever, is that, when considering overseas portfolio investment, the expected *currency trend* is just as important as the expected *market trend*.

22.2 North America

USA – The Dow Jones Industrial Index

	1st January		1st April	1st July	1st October
	US$:£	Index	Index	Index	Index
1976	2.02	852.4	994.1	994.8	979.9
1977	1.70	999.8	927.4	912.6	852.0
1978	1.92	831.2	751.0	812.9	871.4
1979	2.04	805.0	855.3	834.0	872.9
1980	2.22	838.7	784.5	872.3	939.4
1981	2.39	963.9	1014.1	967.7	852.3
1982	1.91	875.0	833.2	803.2	907.2
1983	1.61	1027.0	1130.0	1225.2	1231.1
1984	1.45	1258.6	1153.2	1130.1	1199.0
1985	1.16	1211.6	1272.7	1337.1	1340.9
1986	1.45	1546.7	1790.1	1903.5	

Canada – The Toronto SE Composite Index

	1st January		1st April	1st July	1st October
	C$:£	Index	Index	Index	Index
1976	2.05	973.8	1072.6	1059.4	1041.6
1977	1.72	1012.1	1026.5	1031.2	1002.1
1978	2.11	1059.6	1059.2	1126.2	1290.2
1979	2.42	1310.0	1451.3	1618.4	1753.5
1980	2.60	1813.2	1807.8	2061.3	2228.3
1981	2.85	2268.7	2365.9	2361.1	1902.2
1982	2.26	1954.2	1590.4	1366.8	1591.0
1983	1.99	1985.0	2156.0	2446.9	2466.1
1984	1.80	2552.3	2370.4	2220.9	2379.5
1985	1.53	2400.3	2612.3	2712.5	2650.4
1986	2.03	2900.6	3028.7	3085.5	

22.3 The Far East

Japan – The Tokyo New SE Index

	1st January		1st April	1st July	1st October
	Yen:£	Index	Index	Index	Index
1976	617	323.4	338.4	357.0	356.0
1977	499	383.9	372.8	376.6	389.0
1978	459	364.1	405.2	418.4	434.1
1979	396	449.5	445.6	447.6	462.9
1980	532	459.6	450.4	469.9	490.1
1981	486	491.1	533.8	587.1	543.6
1982	419	570.3	535.7	536.5	520.8
1983	380	593.7	617.7	660.1	692.0
1984	336	731.8	876.6	793.2	822.7
1985	291	913.4	999.3	1029.0	1026.5
1986	288	1047.1	1260.1	1355.7	

Hong Kong – The Hang Seng Bank Index

	1st January		1st April	1st July	1st October
	HK$:£	Index	Index	Index	Index
1976	10.17	350.0	449.5	412.8	413.9
1977	7.96	451.0	424.6	439.6	420.0
1978	8.81	404.0	451.5	567.3	616.9
1979	9.77	495.5	529.5	539.3	677.7
1980	10.99	879.4	784.9	1066.8	1240.6
1981	12.20	1473.5	1387.8	1734.4	1259.2
1982	10.79	1405.8	1174.3	1182.7	862.0
1983	10.46	887.0	996.0	983.7	715.0
1984	11.27	874.9	1024.0	868.6	989.2
1985	9.05	1200.4	1389.1	1570.6	1521.0
1986	11.26	1752.4	1625.9	1733.5	

Singapore – The Straits Times Industrial Index

	1st January		1st April	1st July	1st October
	M$:£	Index	Index	Index	Index
1976	5.03	236.8	254.6	257.9	269.1
1977	4.19	256.2	248.9	256.8	260.3
1978	4.44	264.2	291.3	349.5	359.6
1979	4.40	349.2	371.2	373.7	420.1
1980	4.80	435.4	454.1	544.3	607.6
1981	5.00	660.8	833.3	959.6	642.3
1982	3.89	780.8	726.3	708.4	658.1
1983	3.40	725.4	867.6	971.3	962.8
1984	3.07	1002.0	981.4	894.6	893.4
1985	2.81	812.6	818.2	775.3	769.9
1986	3.05	620.0	594.3	745.9	

22.4 Australia

Australia – The All Ordinary Index

	1st January		1st April	1st July	1st October
	A$:£	Index	Index	Index	Index
1976	1.60	443.1	455.4	476.1	466.3
1977	1.56	431.0	443.3	456.0	431.0
1978	1.67	477.1	458.6	496.7	560.7
1979	1.77	542.0	587.1	583.2	687.8
1980	2.01	740.0	770.9	911.2	992.1
1981	2.02	713.5	707.8	699.9	570.8
1982	1.69	595.5	461.2	470.0	500.4
1983	1.64	485.5	512.7	605.4	711.5
1984	1.61	775.3	749.1	659.0	740.4
1985	1.40	726.1	828.6	860.2	994.2
1986	2.11	1003.8	1131.5	1175.3	

22.5 South Africa

South Africa – The Rand Daily Mail Industrial Index and *The Rand Daily Mail Gold Index*

	1st January		1st April	1st July	1st October
	Rand:£	Index	Index	Index	Index
1976	1.76	212.1	199.6	202.9	189.2
		217.0	*185.6*	*171.8*	*140.8*
1977	1.48	184.3	169.6	177.3	205.1
		169.3	*170.0*	*145.9*	*193.3*
1978	1.67	211.3	203.9	236.2	264.6
		204.7	*203.4*	*215.9*	*255.5*
1979	1.76	268.7	318.0	307.4	374.1
		254.2	*261.9*	*288.0*	*409.9*
1980	1.84	451.2	494.0	545.6	603.5
		530.6	*513.4*	*709.0*	*988.8*
1981	1.78	590.7	620.8	592.9	682.1
		824.5	*642.3*	*479.9*	*687.4*
1982	1.82	701.2	578.9	512.7	685.9
		596.6	*455.8*	*350.4*	*658.2*
1983	1.74	740.9	834.8	959.2	939.1
		988.8	*759.5*	*884.3*	*748.1*
1984	1.77	966.1	1062.3	1026.9	854.0
		887.5	*1002.0*	*989.6*	*1003.1*
1985	2.30	934.7	897.6	1081.8	1074.0
		950.7	*1039.6*	*957.2*	*1098.8*
1986	3.66	1154.5	1272.5	1289.2	
		1156.8	*1157.8*	*1216.4*	

22.6 Continental Europe

Germany – The Commerzbank Index

	1st January		1st April	1st July	1st October
	DM:£	Index	Index	Index	Index
1976	5.30	776.3	805.9	751.7	749.9
1977	4.01	738.6	736.5	750.4	767.8
1978	4.02	794.0	796.4	794.0	852.1
1979	3.71	817.2	778.7	722.2	760.4
1980	3.83	715.7	674.7	724.2	724.4
1981	4.69	683.6	695.7	746.0	675.3
1982	4.29	675.2	722.2	691.4	708.2
1983	3.84	773.2	909.0	957.8	940.5
1984	3.95	1059.7	1022.6	1002.2	1060.0
1985	3.65	1107.9	1183.2	1421.5	1581.3
1986	3.53	1951.5	2105.9	1894.2	

France – The CAC Industrial Index

	1st January		1st April	1st July	1st October
	FFr:£	Index	Index	Index	Index
1976	9.04	63.5	65.1	61.3	53.7
1977	8.43	52.3	44.9	47.8	50.9
1978	8.98	49.2	56.4	63.3	76.5
1979	8.50	71.1	66.3	79.1	95.8
1980	8.92	87.3	86.6	92.3	93.3
1981	10.84	93.3	91.5	63.2	73.6
1982	10.88	100.0	102.1	97.1	96.1
1983	10.88	93.1	116.1	128.3	143.5
1984	12.08	158.9	167.1	173.6	178.9
1985	11.17	180.2	207.9	214.4	210.2
1986	10.85	243.3	312.1	320.1	

Switzerland – The Swiss Bank Index

	1st January		1st April	1st July	1st October
	SwFr:£	Index	Index	Index	Index
1976	5.30	281.5	289.9	297.5	275.0
1977	4.16	289.7	289.6	297.7	316.6
1978	3.81	301.1	293.9	291.6	280.2
1979	3.30	289.2	316.4	312.1	323.6
1980	3.54	302.7	282.6	303.7	306.2
1981	4.25	299.4	302.3	288.9	249.6
1982	3.43	258.5	257.6	243.0	252.8
1983	3.24	294.5	314.2	332.7	334.3
1984	3.16	383.8	369.7	361.3	375.3
1985	3.01	385.8	414.3	447.9	481.0
1986	2.97	587.9	593.8	557.9	

Netherlands – The Amsterdam Industrial Index

	1st January		1st April	1st July	1st October
	FI:£	Index	Index	Index	Index
1976	5.43	96.6	100.8	90.1	81.0
1977	4.18	83.4	86.6	84.3	76.4
1978	4.35	80.9	76.4	83.1	88.5
1979	4.02	80.7	77.5	74.0	73.6
1980	4.22	68.4	61.1	61.5	60.6
1981	5.09	61.6	68.4	74.1	64.6
1982	4.70	63.1	71.9	67.1	68.7
1983	4.25	83.6	108.4	110.6	116.0
1984	4.44	133.9	131.5	126.4	135.8
1985	4.12	145.3	165.0	179.4	189.9
1986	3.98	242.5	253.6	284.4	

22.7 The United Kingdom *(for comparison)*

UK – The Financial Times Industrial Ordinary Index

	1st January	1st April	1st July	1st October
	Index	Index	Index	Index
1976	375.7	398.8	386.5	317.5
1977	354.7	412.5	451.2	520.1
1978	485.4	462.5	458.1	499.2
1979	470.9	532.2	475.1	466.8
1980	414.2	432.4	461.4	483.2
1981	474.5	529.8	548.7	475.0
1982	530.4	570.1	549.3	579.4
1983	596.7	655.1	709.8	703.7
1984	775.7	870.8	822.1	856.9
1985	952.8	963.8	952.5	1004.8
1986	1131.4	1402.2	1373.7	

22.8 Interpreting the indices

The index listings and exchange rates contained in sections 22.2 – 22.7 can be used to produce a good deal of statistical information about the performance of the various markets and currencies since 1975. However, the most salient statistic from a UK investor's point of view is the performance of an index – as a broad measure of a market – between specified dates, adjusted to sterling terms. Such an adjustment effectively measures the change in value of an investment of a sterling sum in a hypothetical overseas equity which moves exactly in line with its domestic market index, thus establishing a yardstick against which actual sterling investments in the same or UK or other markets can be compared.

The information contained in sections 22.2–22.7 allows for currency-adjusted index comparisons at 1st January 1975–1985 only for illustrative purposes, but the adjustment procedure given below can be applied to any index and currency, between any two dates:

Step 1
Ascertain the index numbers on the selected dates.
Step 2
Ascertain the corresponding foreign currency/sterling exchange rate on the selected dates and convert to a sterling expression by dividing 100p by these rates. The result will be the value in pence of one basic unit of the foreign currency in question on each of these two dates. Then calculate the percentage change in the latter from the base date (the first selected date) to the second selected date.
Step 3
Adjust the index number on the second selected date by the percentage change (up or down) found in *Step 2*.

Example

To compare the performance of the Dow Jones Industrial Index (United States) and the Tokyo New SE Index (Japan) between 1st January 1982 and 1st January 1985, in sterling terms.

Step 1 – Index numbers

	USA	Japan
1.1.82 (Base date)	875.0	570.3
	=(+38.5%)	=(+60.2%)
1.1.85	1211.6	913.4

Step 2 – Currencies

	USA	Japan
1.1.82	$1=52.3p (100p ÷ 1.91)	¥1=0.239p (100p ÷ 419)
	(+64.8%)	(+43.9%)
1.1.85	$1=86.2p (100p ÷ 1.16)	¥1=0.344p (100p ÷ 291)

Step 3 – Adjustment of 1.1.85 index numbers

	USA	Japan
1.1.82	875.0	570.3
(Base date)		
	= (+**128.2%**)	= (+**130.5%**)
1.1.85	1996.7 (1211.6 plus 64.8%)	1314.4 (913.4 plus 43.9%)

This example illustrates well the effects of the interaction of market and currency movements on foreign investments by UK residents. It shows that, while the Dow Jones Industrial Index performed far less well than the Tokyo SE Index during the period, the greater strength of the United States dollar against sterling almost completely closed the gap when the two are compared in sterling adjusted terms.

To arrive at the true performance of an overseas index from a UK investor's point of view over a period commencing – and if desired, ending – prior to 24th October 1979, it would, strictly speaking, be necessary further to adjust the index numbers for the investment currency premium ruling on the selected dates. However, since the premium is no longer a relevant consideration such further adjustment would be of limited historical interest and the procedure necessary does not warrant pursuit in this book. A simple adjustment of an index to reflect the change in value of sterling as shown above will be quite sufficient to underline the point made in section 22.1 and which bears repetition here: when considering overseas portfolio investment, the expected currency trend is as important as the expected market trend.

Section 23
Investment planning

23.1 Getting investment advice

Investment planning is such a subjective issue that no book could ever give specific advice – that is, put forward a portfolio of named investments – which it could claim to be irrefutably valid for ever more. Hopefully, however, this guide has demonstrated that most, if not all, investment media have drawbacks, or even outright disadvantages in certain circumstances, as well as their usually much more prominently emphasised benefits. Always remember that investment products, like goods in a shop window, are there to be sold by the 'vendors' and will inevitably be 'packaged' or promoted in such a way as to have the maximum impact on potential buyers – in this case the investing public.

This leads on to what should be the overriding message to emerge from this book: seek reputable and regular professional advice if you really want your money to stand the best chance of working to your maximum advantage. This piece of advice itself is not offered without reason, although it must be said straight-away that there are many private investors, well versed in the ways of money, who are entirely capable of managing their investments independently, often with a great deal of success. Yet evidence suggests that if left to their own devices many more make what can only be described as rash investment decisions, without investigating fully the implications of what they are doing, or the alternatives open to them.

This is not to say that all investment advisers will offer truly unbiased advice, while even the most impartial will make recommendations which fail to live up to expectations, no matter how soundly based or carefully reasoned their advice at the time. However, if the adviser is at all competent he should at least know what is a suitable investment, or mix of investments, in given circumstances. The question is, of course, how do you decide which, of the wide choice available, is the right advisory service for your particular situation? The answer will depend very much on what sort of advice you are seeking – for example, is it likely to be occasional guidance, or do you want a comprehensive investment management 'package'? Moreover, the amount of money you have available will be an important determining factor.

Whatever your position, however, the first thing to consider is the range of services offered by a stockbroker. These are covered in some detail in section 2. None the less, it is worth emphasising here that you can get a broker's opinion on most investment matters simply by calling at the 'securities' counter of your bank branch. Many broking firms have a special department dealing full time with the investment enquiries and stock market transactions of bank customers who do not maintain direct contact with a broker themselves. Indeed, the full range of a broker's private client services may be made available to 'regular' customers. This is a useful facility for the new or smaller investor seeking advice that will be as impartial as it is possible to obtain anywhere today.

Other advisory services tend to be of the complete 'package' variety referred to earlier. For example, all the 'High Street' banks and many merchant banks have investment divisions which provide a comprehensive service, usually with a choice between non-discretionary (with prior consultation) and discretionary (no consultation) portfolio management. The minimum sum accepted is in some cases quite high, while the management charge will vary from bank to bank and depend upon the facilities provided and the size of the underlying portfolio. It may be reduced if investments are held in the bank's 'in-house' products, e.g. unit trusts (see section 11.5).

The services provided by stockbrokers and banks are by no means the full range open to the investing public. For example, a number of unit trust groups and other investment houses now offer a private portfolio management service (naturally based on their own products), while many leading insurance brokers, accountants and solicitors will provide investment advice for their clients (although the Financial Services Bill proposals, that all investment businesses should be registered with appropriately qualified advisers, may restrict the ability of many such firms or individuals to give advice). However, this latter type of service is usually highly 'personalised' and not many would claim to offer the all-round expertise and facilities found in a stockbroking firm or a bank's investment division. In many cases, in fact, the investment portfolio will be managed with regular guidance from a stockbroker.

There is one other category of advisory service which should be mentioned here – the 'independent' investment manager or management company. This is an expanding area of the invest-ment management business, but it is not regulated to any effective extent. Indeed, this lack of regulation was a major driving force behind the Financial Services Bill now before Parliament (see section 1.3). Thus, and while it must be said that there are some very capable and reputable advisers acting independently, this was an avenue where an investor could be exposed to the actions of a less scrupulous minority. The organisation may be anything from a one-man business upwards and may offer a comprehen-sive or very specialist service. Generally speaking, this sort of service is for the investor seeking what is normally active portfolio management but, before entering into an agreement, make sure that you know what you are getting and check the credentials of the business as thoroughly as you can.

Inevitably, there are some advisers, or people purporting to be advisers, whose counsel you should generally disregard or at best treat with reservation, at least until you have obtained a second opinion. The important thing is not to sign anything or to part with any money until you are completely satisfied that you are dealing with a reputable organisation and that the investment programme proposed is right for you. So, beware of:

i   Door-to-door and telephone salespeople wanting to talk to you 'about investment'. The probability is that the person will be selling single-premium bonds of the type described in section 12. Quite often these will be the products of highly reputable insurance companies, but it is their *application* which is all-important and they are most certainly not 'right' for all investors – although the salesperson sitting beside you may not see it that way.

ii   Unsolicited investment propositions through the post. The

144 The Stock Market

'mail-shot' is a popular investment-selling technique. For example, anyone can gain access to a UK company's share register and thus will have a ready-made mailing list of known investors; a big company may have tens of thousands of shareholders. In particular, watch out for specific share recommendations emanating from foreign sources.

iii   Advice from any source other than recognised investment advisers, including family, friends, business acquaintances and, especially, the 'chap in the local'. Remember, what may be right for them is not necessarily right for you, no matter how well intentioned – or convincing – their 'advice'.

iv   Tip-sheets. There has been a proliferation in the number of 'tip-sheets' – investment letters available on a subscription basis and written by stock market analysts – in recent years. It must be said that some of these can claim to make, or to have made, some astute recommendations although their often wide circulation does mean that these are on occasions self-feeding. The point is that most of their 'tips' are shares in which there is a relatively narrow market and a sudden rush of buying orders will push the share price up sharply – see also section 14.1. This is not to say that tip sheets do not have their place; in fact, they often alert investors to interesting situations that might otherwise have gone unnoticed. None the less, if you want to participate, set aside a sensible proportion – say, not more than 10% – of your capital for this generally speculative purpose and do not let it encroach on the main body of your portfolio. The publishers of tip-sheets will be required to register as investment businesses under the provisions of the Financial Services Bill.

Finally, a word about the financial press, on whose articles so many investment decisions are based. Many national newspapers with influential financial pages – for example the *Daily Telegraph, Daily Mail, The Times,* their Sunday equivalents and, of course, the *Financial Times* – have regular features devoted to personal financial planning and investment, apart from their daily reports on markets and company news. In addition, there are the excellent weekly publications, *Financial Weekly* and *Investors Chronicle.* These all provide valuable information and guidance on financial matters and are especially useful for keeping abreast of new developments on the investment scene. Indeed, the 'City' pages are compulsory reading for professional advisers and investors and should also be for anyone with even a passing interest in their investments. However, use them principally as a source of ideas to discuss with a stockbroker or other adviser – don't try and put together, and administer independently, a portfolio of investments selected at random from your newspaper.

To summarise, in the final analysis it is your money and you must invest it as you see fit. But the business of investment can be a minefield for the unwary and nowhere is it more true to say that there is no substitute for good advice.

23.2 Constructing an investment portfolio

Section 23.1 discussed in broad outline the various ways in which an investor can go about getting investment advice. However, most people understandably like to have a say in how, and in what, their money is invested. Indeed, the whole purpose of this guide is to help and encourage investors to take a more know-ledgeable interest in their investments.

So, just how does one set about constructing an investment portfolio? As ever, its final 'shape' will depend on the underlying circumstances, the investment objectives and the amount of money available. A quick read through section 2.1 may help here. Of course, the very concept of portfolio planning – and investment management generally – would be entirely super-fluous if there was, somewhere, an investment which combined the highest possible rate of interest with the guarantee of substantial capital appreciation but which carried no risk and no liability to any form of taxation. Needless to say, no such investment exits, nor ever will, but many investors still start out with what virtually amount to these criteria! The first thing to come to terms with is that you can't have your investment 'cake' and eat it.

If there is a generally accepted rule of thumb when looking at the stock market and, indeed, other investments, it is of the 'swings and roundabouts' variety; investments giving a high immediate income (or yield) generally have comparatively limited or questionable capital and/or income growth potential while, on the other hand, those regarded as attractive for the latter purpose will usually offer a lower initial income. This should be qualified by one further premise; the higher the potential reward, the higher the risk.

The next step is to decide which of the following descriptions of three different 'categories' of investor most closely accords with your own philosophy; you cannot be all three 'undiluted', but you can, if you wish, accommodate a portion of each:

i   Depositor (ultra-conservative).
ii Genuine investor (taking a sensible long-term view).
iii Speculator (prepared to take a high risk for a hopefully high reward).

If you fall totally and intractably into categories (i) or (iii) then it must be said that the rest of this section may be of limited further interest to you. In the former case, simply depositing money with a bank, a building society, or whatever, for an indefinite term, does not really constitute investment planning, unless one is taking a highly pessimistic view of investment markets generally (but see section 2.1). In the case of (iii), you clearly do not have the temperament or inclination to bother with long-term investment planning. But, optimistic newcomers beware – 'playing the market', whether by self-selection, tip-sheets, 'stagging' new issues, technical analysis (the prediction of share price movements based on a chart of past performance) or whatever, is not the way to an easy fortune. It will occupy a great deal of time, require a mixture of discipline, bravado and, most of all, good luck, with, preferably, the close co-operation of a professional 'on the scene' – a difficult combination to achieve all at once, with the likelihood of much frustration and disappointment along the way.

The key to successful portfolio planning lies in achieving balance and diversification within a compact range of well selected, top quality investments. It does not require the accumulation of a vast quantity of individual holdings (you might just as well save yourself the trouble and put it all into a single, broadly-based, unit trust). For most private portfolios there is no reason why any one investment should represent less than 5% of the total amount invested or, put another way, 20 holdings is usually sufficient for a portfolio under £100,000. This number could very well drop to perhaps 15 for £50,000 down to £30,000 and 10 for less than £30,000. As a general rule, aim to invest a minimum of £2,000 in any one holding; hence the great attraction of managed funds (see section 11) for sums of less than, say, £20,000. If, parallel to your main portfolio holdings, you wish to run a 'fun' portfolio of speculative stocks (not more than 10% of your total investment worth, remember) by all means do so but, to repeat a point made in section 23.1, do not let it encroach on your main portfolio – at least until your dealing prowess consistently surpasses that of the professionals!

But what exactly is meant by 'balance' and 'diversification'? Well, nobody can ever be sure what is around the corner and nowhere is this more true than in financial markets, even though professional advisers and their teams of economists and analysts spend much time and effort consulting their crystal ball in an attempt to forecast what *is* going to happen, either to the markets generally or, for example, to the shares of a particular company. Thus, it is only sensible to spread the risk by holding a reasonable number of different investments, whether directly or indirectly, e.g. via managed funds.

Concentrating your capital on a single investment or just a few holdings may make a lot of money for you if you have selected perfectly; but, remember, if your judgement proves to be fallible, the reverse is also true. In other words, don't keep all your eggs in one basket. 'Balance' will come from dividing the portfolio into sensible proportions between different media, a prime example being Government stocks and equities, to reflect a chosen investment policy, and 'diversification' from spreading the capital so allocated between different investments within each medium. It is probably best to pursue this with an example of a fairly typical situation.

Example

Suppose that in September 1986 an investor with no previous experience of the Stock Exchange has £50,000 to invest for the long term. His life assurance and pension arrangements are adequate and his earned income is sufficient for his everyday needs, being taxed at the basic rate of 29%, although it is on the verge of moving into the higher (40%) band. He is retaining a margin of liquidity (£3,000) on deposit to cover any incidental capital expenditure and has £5,000 already invested in National Savings Certificates ('NSCs') which he is going to keep. After discussing the matter with a stockbroker, it is decided that the money will be invested primarily for capital appreciation, but with a moderate income. The only proviso is that £5,000–£10,000 may be required in about two years' time to put towards a holiday cottage. The following portfolio is recommended to him:

i   British Government stocks
   £10,000 (20%) in a low coupon stock redeemable in 1989.
   £5,000 (10%) in a higher coupon stock redeemable in
   ————   1994 (under par and ex dividend).
   £15,000 (30%)

ii UK 'blue-chip' equities
   £2,500 (5%) in each of six shares. The companies selected were leaders in their particular sectors, having good management, a record of consistent earnings and dividend growth, a strong balance sheet and operating in industries where long-term growth can be anticipated.
   £15,000 (30%)

iii Unit trusts invested in UK companies
   £3,750 (7½%) in a trust specialising in 'recovery' shares.
   £3,750 (7½%) in a trust specialising in small companies.
   £7,500 (15%)

iv Unit trusts invested in overseas markets
   £3,750 (7½%) in a broadly-based American trust.
   £2,500 (5%) in a broadly-based Japanese trust.
   £2,500 (5%) in a trust specialising in high technology shares, mostly American and Japanese.
   £3,750 (7½%) in a trust specialising in natural resource shares.
   £12,500 (25%)

   £50,000 (100%) spread over 15 investments.

If this portfolio is analysed, the all round balance and diversification it achieves becomes readily apparent. Firstly, consider the balance. The overall emphasis has been placed on equities, because the primary objective is long-term capital growth. Yet there is £15,000 in the gilt-edged market, with its more defensive properties, supported by the NSCs in the background. So, ignoring the £3,000 liquidity reserve, the investor has around one-third of his total capital in non-equity holdings. This is usually about the right sort of balance (between investments of this nature and equities) to aim for when establishing a private investment portfolio where the background situation resembles that of this example, although, inevitably, some adjustment to the proportions may be deemed necessary from time to time.

Secondly, the diversification. Overall, there is a high degree of diversification within this portfolio, despite the fact that there are only 15 holdings. This is particularly true of the equity investments, where the six individual shareholdings and six unit trusts cover a wide range of markets, sectors and companies, either directly or indirectly. In addition, there is a good geographical spread, with one quarter allocated to overseas markets.

However, it is not a question of simply choosing at random a range of investments covering as many different areas as one can think of. Moreover, the more cautious investor might think twice about committing two-thirds of the portfolio to equity markets, while the more aggressively minded probably would say that an investment programme like this is too 'neutral', that its broad diversification does not commit it enough to one view. But these would be the attitudes of investors from, or verging on, categories (i) and (iii) – see page 146 – for whom, yes, the portfolio would need to be adjusted. This is where, against the backcloth of the prevailing investment climate, the adviser must assimilate his knowledge, as in this example, of the various vehicles that might be suitable in given circumstances, before submitting his recommendations to the client.

So, given that the portfolio in this example was selected for a typical 'middle-of-the-road' investor, what was the 'thinking' behind it? The broker's letter (with a liberal dosage of author's licence) to the client might have read something like this:

September 1986

Dear Client,

Further to our meeting, I am enclosing, for your final approval, a summary of my specific recommendations for the investment of £50,000. The portfolio has been constructed along the lines we discussed and I believe it would be in a strong position to provide you with the capital growth which you will be seeking in the coming years, subject to the occasional alteration to reflect changes in the investment climate. Importantly, however, there is scope for a steadily increasing dividend income and I have not overlooked the fact that you may need up to £10,000 in about two years' time for a holiday cottage.

Since you do manage comfortably on your earnings and, bearing in mind that a high investment income would probably take you into the 40% tax band, the immediate return from the portfolio is a little below average. However, if you find that you are short of income at any time it would always be possible to realise the occasional capital profit or, as a last resort, to uplift the yield level on a permanent basis. While on the subject of taxation, I explained that capital profits are generally more valuable than taxable income, especially income liable to more than the basic rate. This is because the maximum rate of capital gains tax is 30%, although the first £6,300 of net gains realised in the current (1986/87) tax year is exempt from charge altogether – this after providing for an indexation allowance. This 'exemption' will be increased by the rate of inflation in future years. In addition, all capital profits realised on British Government securities will be free from charge to capital gains tax. Thus, there is considerable scope for manoeuvre each year before a liability to capital gains tax arises.

You asked me to recap briefly on the reasoning behind my proposals and, since these are weighted towards equity markets, with about two-thirds of the capital allocated to shares and unit trusts, I will start with this subject. You observed quite correctly during our discussion that in recent years many leading shares failed to fulfil their traditional role of providing a hedge against inflation. As an isolated statement this is undeniable, but there were special factors acting as a negative influence in many areas of industry and commerce throughout much of the 1970s, in particular, and this was reflected in a correspondingly turbulent equity market during that decade. Moreover, the counter argument is not only that there were very many shares which, over the same period, achieved a rate of growth well in excess of inflation, but also that none of the alternatives which one might realistically have considered for portfolio investment has fared any better.

The fundamental case for equities is really quite simple. In a free economy, companies trade in a competitive environment, hopefully increasing their assets and their profitability, and thus the dividends paid to their proprietors. This, in turn, will lead in the long run to a steady increase in share values. Of course, the very nature of competition means that some will do better than others and some might even go out of business but, although that is the ultimate risk, it is normally signalled in advance by a deterioration in the company's trading position. In any event, by applying certain criteria to the selection of one's equity investments and by keeping the portfolio under regular observation, the threat of ending up a shareholder in what few failures there are among companies listed on The Stock Exchange is small.

This brings me to the particular equity investments which I have selected for your portfolio. In the first place, I have chosen the shares of six UK 'blue-chip' companies which are leaders in their respective fields of activity. The criteria on which they were chosen is that they should (i) be demonstrably well managed, (ii) have a record of consistent earnings and dividend growth, with a strong balance sheet and (iii) operate in, and be seen to be expanding in, industries where long-term growth opportunities clearly exist. You may have expected me, as a stockbroker, to put forward a list of shares I regard as 'recovery' situations, the next 'high fliers', takeover-bid candidates or whatever, but the chances of any adviser picking out a handful of 'winners' are remote and you would probably end up with a poor quality portfolio and a performance to match. Having said that, there are undoubtedly interesting investment opportunities to be found amongst such 'special situations' but for a portfolio such as yours, it is better to obtain a broad coverage of these via one or two specialised unit trusts. If you decide that you really would like to have a modest 'flutter' now and again in something speculative, I suggest you separate it from the main body of your investments, perhaps even to the extent of allocating it to a subsidiary portfolio designated 'portfolio B'. Otherwise, the evidence is overwhelming; a limited range of well selected, top quality growth shares, based on the criteria described above, will almost certainly perform better than any other equity portfolio strategy in the long run. I can assure you that it is completely fallacious to believe that, just because a company is big, its share price action will necessarily lack in performance. This, then, is the basis on which I have selected the six UK shares, with 30% of the capital available to be divided equally between them.

I have then chosen a range of six unit trusts to cover markets, or sectors of markets, which I would like to see represented within your portfolio because of their long-term potential and the diversification they provide, but which it would be difficult to achieve through individual equity holdings with the capital you have available. I have made already a passing reference to the interesting opportunities to be found amongst 'recovery' situ-

ations and said that in a portfolio of this size I believe an interest in such shares can best be taken via a managed fund. I take the same view of investment in the shares of small companies and thus I have earmarked a further 15% of your capital for two unit trusts specialising in these categories to complement the six UK 'blue-chip' equities.

The four remaining unit trusts, to which I have allocated a further 25%, would provide you with a significant exposure to overseas markets, particularly America and Japan, which are, of course, two very important economies with stock markets substantially larger than the UK's. Moreover, both offer investment opportunities not readily available in this country. As a result, expert knowledge and investment management, via the medium of unit trusts, is to be particularly recommended. In addition to two trusts giving a broadly-based coverage of each market, I am recommending one specialising in the shares of companies engaged in high technology, these being mostly American and Japanese, and one with a portfolio concentrating on companies involved in the production and processing of natural resources, this being invested on a wider geographical basis. These latter sectors contain outstanding, but often higher-risk, investment opportunities and I believe that for an investor in your position the 'wider spread, lower risk' approach offered by a unit trust is a more sensible way of achieving an interest in both than backing one or two 'horses' in each, bearing in mind that the normal considerations of risk that this entails would be compounded by the added degree of unpredictability (for different reasons, of course) that is so often associated with high technology and the exploitation of natural resources.

This concludes my comments on my equity proposals and I would like to turn now to the remaining recommendations, the two Government stocks. These are the 'bankers' of the portfolio in the event of something going dramatically and unexpectedly wrong in the equity market. I have chosen two stocks, each of which will fulfil a specific but different purpose.

The low coupon 'short' has considerable defensive properties and will provide a measure of liquidity in an emergency, or if an outstanding investment opportunity presents itself at a later date. Its price represents a substantial discount to its guaranteed redemption value of 100 in 1989 and the most likely expectation is that the price will rise steadily to reflect this as the maturity date draws nearer – its already fairly close proximity means that there is only a limited risk that the price will slip back and, even then, this would be, perforce, only a temporary setback. Ultimately, therefore, this stock provides the prospect of a calculable capital gain, come what may, with only a small taxable income. As I have already said, the gain will be free of capital gains tax, underlining the attraction of low coupon stocks to investors whose income tax liabilities may extend beyond the basic rate.

That my second selection is a higher coupon stock, with the prospect of negligible capital growth if it is held right through to maturity in 1994, may seem at variance with my last comment. However, I am mindful of the fact that you said you would like to achieve a moderate income from the portfolio and, since my other proposals are geared largely to the provision of capital growth, this investment would give the overall income level a useful boost. Morever, medium and longer dated stocks are more sensitive generally to movements in interest rates than short-dated stocks and, if rates should fall, the price of the stock could very well move above 100, giving you the option to realise a capital profit well before redemption. Indeed, it is normally sensible to do this since retaining (or buying) a stock above 100, with a view to holding it until redemption, means that part of the capital value then existing is being sacrificed to provide an income. This is why I have selected a stock which stands below par and, incidentally, I have been careful to choose one which is available in ex-dividend form, this presenting, as a general rule, the most advantageous buying opportunity.

You will appreciate that it might be necessary to adjust the permutation of high coupon, low coupon and index-linked stocks, as well as short and long maturities, from time to time, to reflect changes in interest rate and inflationary expectations. For the record, however, there are few, if any, circumstances under which I would recommend irredeemable stocks as a portfolio investment. I have suggested that 30% of the portfolio should be divided equally between these stocks but I would just make the point that the proportion in Government guaranteed securities would be rather higher by virtue of your holding of National Savings Certificates. You will appreciate that with the short-dated Government stock and the National Savings Certificates – giving you starting capital of £15,000 in a readily realisable form – your potential cash requirement for the holiday cottage will be well covered, if, at any time, it seems better not to disturb any of your equity holdings.

I trust my comments will assist you in reaching your final decision and I look forward to hearing from you.

Yours sincerely

A Broker

It must be emphasised, firstly, that this example is intended for illustration purposes only and does not constitute a standing recommendation for a portfolio where the circumstances of a reader resemble those on which it is based and secondly, that there may be a wide divergence of opinion between different advisers about the 'best' solution for any particular investor at any particular time.

Hopefully, however, this section has demonstrated that constructing an investment portfolio does require careful planning and that it is best undertaken in consultation with an expert. None the less, it also contains some guidelines – stated or implied – which might be of help to those investors determined to 'go it alone'.

23.3 Suggested suitability ratings

The purpose of this section is to suggest a 'suitability rating' for the principal investment areas open to the private investor today in five different circumstances, which should assist new or, indeed, existing, investors to arrive at a sensible investment policy. For easy reference, these circumstances and ratings are set out in the tables below and opposite. It will be noticed that the circumstances are based primarily on the tax position of the investor, with the 'requirements' simply being typical within the particular tax range.

The 'circumstances'

	1	2	3	4	5
Tax class (Suggested range)	Nil (0%)	Basic (29%)	Middle (40%-50%)*	High (55%-60%)*	Non resident (Exempt)
Requirements	Income	Income/ growth	Mainly growth	Growth	Income/ growth

* Top marginal liability.

The 'ratings'

Circumstances	1	2	3	4	5
Investment category:					
Fixed interest					
Gilt-edged securities:					
i High coupon for income	A1*1	A1	B	X	A1*2
ii Low coupon or index-linked	X	A	A1	A1	X
Industrial debentures/unsecured loans	X	B	B	X	X
Convertible loans	X	B	B	X	X
Preference shares/irredeemable stocks	X	X	X	X	X
Foreign currency bonds	X	B	B	B	A
Equity					
Direct shareholdings in selected:					
i Market leaders	X	A1	A1	A1	A
ii Smaller companies	X	B	A	A	B
iii Overseas companies	X	B	A	A	A
UK managed funds (inc. unit trusts)					
i Income/general funds	A1	A1	B	B	X
ii Growth/specialised sector funds	X	A1	A1	A1	X
iii Overseas funds	X	A1	A1	A1	X
iv Gilt funds	B	B	B	X	X
Offshore funds (exc. currency funds)	B	B	B	B	A1
Property or other single premium bonds	X	B	A	A	X
Other					
National Savings Deposits	A1	B	X	X	A
National Savings Certificates	X	A	A1	A1	X
Channel Islands-based currency funds:					
i Sterling 'roll-up' funds	X	B	X	X	A
ii Foreign currency funds	X	B	B	B	A
Building society (as a 'permanent' investment)	X	B	X	X	X
Gold (coins, etc.)	X	A	A	A	A

*1 = National Savings Bank registered Government stocks.
*2 = UK tax exempt Government stocks.

Key to symbols
A1 = Normally highly recommended in the circumstances.
A = Suitable for inclusion in a portfolio to supplement those rated A1.
B = Might be considered in certain circumstances.
X = Considered unsuitable in the circumstances.

The ratings are really self-explanatory. Those categories rated A1 should, it is suggested, ideally form the nucleus of a long-term investment portfolio in the various circumstances, supplemented, if appropriate, by those rated A and, perhaps, B. Those rated X should preferably be avoided and it is hoped that investors with any investments rated X will at least consider switching the capital involved into an area more likely to be suited to their circumstances. No attempt has been made to (i) distinguish between income and growth within the various investment categories, except where indicated, (ii) suggest suitable proportions for a portfolio of investments, or (iii) select individual investments within each category, as all these considerations will depend on the individual's requirements and the prevailing investment climate (see section 23.2). It is also acknowledged that any category could become relatively more or less attractive from time to time as a result of market movements and changes in economic expectations or tax legislation.

Section 24

A brief history of
The Stock Exchange, London

1553   The first known 'company' to establish a system of public shares was founded. The 'Russian Company', as it was called, was set up to find the North-East Passage under the leadership of merchant venturer Sebastian Cabot. £6,000 was raised to finance the expedition by selling shares at £5 each.

1568   The first recorded dealings in shares and the origins of the jobber/broker system.

Late   During this period a market in stocks and shares was
1500s   gradually established with brokers operating from coffee
to   houses in the Threadneedle Street area. Details of the
1773   various enterprises in which shares were offered were posted on boards in the coffee houses, and waiters acted as messengers between dealers. To the present day, The Stock Exchange attendants are still known as *waiters*.

1670   The Hudson's Bay Company (full title: The Governor and Company of Adventurers of England trading into Hudson's Bay) was formed by Royal Charter. This is the oldest company still quoted on The Stock Exchange, although it is now Canadian domiciled.

1694   The Bank of England was established as a joint-stock company by a group of London merchants to lend money to the state and deal with the National Debt. It was eventually brought into public ownership in 1946.

1720   The year of the 'South Sea Bubble'. Set up with capital raised by selling shares, the South Sea Company was originally intended to establish trade with South America. The venture lost money from the start but, instead of ceasing to trade, more and more shares were sold to the public, who were deluded into thinking all was well. Eventually the 'bubble' burst and a great many subscribers to the venture suffered financial loss. The 'Bubble Act' was subsequently passed in the same year as a safeguard against a similar fraud.

Early   The Government, recognising the success achieved by
1700s   commercial ventures in raising money from the public, decided to use the system to fund its own expenditure. So the issue of gilt-edged securities began, providing a more secure alternative to the risk of company stocks.

1773   Dealings in stocks and shares had expanded to the point where a centralised market was desirable. A dwelling house in Threadneedle Street was acquired for the purpose by the 'coffee house' stockbrokers and named 'The Stock Exchange'. Even today, The Stock Exchange trading floor is often referred to as *The House*.

1801   The first purpose-built Stock Exchange was erected by its members on the site of the present building.

1812   The Stock Exchange achieved official recognition and the first Stock Exchange Rule Book was issued.

Early   The Industrial Revolution was under way, with The
1800s   Stock Exchange, for the first time since the South Sea Bubble, once again accepted as the most efficient method of raising capital from the public. In particular, it played a major role in financing the building of Britain's railways, the 'railway boom' marking one of the biggest waves of investment in the history of The Stock Exchange.

Late   Another major investment wave, this time in South
1800s African gold mines – the 'Kaffir boom' – and The Stock
       Exchange entered the twentieth century as the world's
       principal security market.

Early   The First World War, the 1920–21 depression and the
1900s   celebrated Wall Street crash of 1929 combined to make
        this an extremely difficult period for investors and The
        Stock Exchange alike. Although the late 1930s saw an
        economic recovery and a then record turnover in Stock
        Exchange securities, further disruptions were brought
        about by the Second World War.

1940s   In the post-war years up to the early 1960s, Stock
to   Exchange activity increased steadily as the UK economy
1979   gradually expanded and living standards rose. However,
        the late 1960s and 1970s saw the economy move from
        crisis to crisis with a sharply accelerating rate of inflation
        which, at one time, reached an annualised rate of over
        20%. In turn, these unstable conditions engendered a
        volatile stock market including, in 1974, the most severe
        'bear' market seen for decades.

1972   The present Stock Exchange was completed on the site of
        the original building. It took six years to construct, at a
        cost of £15 million.

Early   Against a backcloth of the most severe industrial
1980s   recession since the 1920s and a continuing unsettled
        international economic and political climate, the 1980s
        hardly got off to an inspiring start. But, as ever, stock
        market investors were soon looking ahead to better
        times. With North Sea oil in full flow and a Government
        committed to (i) reducing state borrowings and its indus-
        trial participation and (ii) promoting free enterprise,
        share prices overall reached new peak levels in April
        1986 as the domestic and other major world economies
        turned around and entered a new phase of growth.

1986   The year of the 'Big Bang' and perhaps the most
        significant in the entire history of The Stock Exchange
        (see sections 1.2 and 1.3).

and
the
future?
Important developments in the reshaping UK securities industry will continue for some time to come. For example, the Financial Services Bill will be enacted in 1987, while in September 1986 proposals were announced for the merger of The Stock Exchange with the International Securities Regulatory Organisation to create a new Stock Exchange, The International Stock Exchange of the United Kingdom and the Republic of Ireland.

Meanwhile, in 1987 The Stock Exchange will be enhancing its new dealing system and pricing service (SEAQ), to include an automatic small transaction execution facility. Other plans on the horizon include a computerised 'book entry' transfer system designed to speed up and simplify the present method of share transfer between seller and buyer.

It would be presumptuous to try to forecast what effect all this will have on private investors. Nonetheless, the signs are promising; the costs of investing in the stock market look like falling and, certainly, the 'investor in the street' is becoming an increasingly important target market for the investment industry.

Supplement

Taxation and the investor

The tax year commences on 6th April and ends on the following 5th April.

A comprehensive coverage of the UK tax system would require a sizeable volume alone and, indeed, several publications dealing solely with personal taxation are readily available. However, as tax considerations play a major part in investment planning, no investment handbook could be complete without reference to the subject. This supplement, therefore, contains a summary of those aspects of taxation which are most likely to affect or interest the private investor.

The supplement has been up-dated to include the relevant changes in personal tax legislation for the tax year 1986/7.

It is recommended that investors seek specialist advice if in doubt as to their existing or potential tax position when making investment decisions.

Note: Reference to the following aspects of taxation will be found in the sections indicated:

	Section
Takeover bids and mergers – capital gains tax considerations	8.5
Insurance-linked (single premium) bonds – a summary of their tax treatment	12.2
Gold coins – a summary of their tax treatment	20.4

Section S1

Income tax

S1.1 Main personal allowances

Main personal allowances

	Allowance 1986/87
Single person	£2,335
Married person	£3,655
Wife's earnings	£2,335
One-parent family	£3,655
Age allowances:*	
Single person	£2,850
Married person	£4,505

*For persons over 65 years of age. Where total income exceeds £9,400, the allowance is gradually reduced to that applicable to persons under 65.

S1.2 Income tax rates

Income tax rates

Taxable income	Tax rate 1986/87
Basic rate	
First £17,200	29%
Higher rates	
£17,201 – £20,200	40%
£20,201 – £25,400	45%
£25,401 – £33,300	50%
£33,301 – £41,200	55%
Excess over £41,200	60%

S1.3 Accrued interest on fixed-interest securities

The Finance Act 1985 contained measures to counter 'bondwashing', a practice whereby investors could capitalise the gross interest accrued in a fixed-interest security by selling it prior to the ex dividend date and thus avoid a liability to income tax on it.

With effect from 28th February 1986, the interest accrued in respect of the relevant interest period, calculated on a day-to-day basis, will be segregated from the capital element for income tax purposes. In this way, the seller or transferor will incur a liability to income tax on the accrued interest so realised. By extension, the buyer or transferee will be entitled to relief in respect of accrued interest 'acquired' as part of an investment in a fixed-interest security.

This provision extends to British Government securities, marketable local authority stocks and bonds, industrial debenture and loan stocks and all similar marketable securities on which interest is deemed to accrue on a day-to-day basis. However, individuals whose total holdings of qualifying securities do not exceed £5,000 in nominal value at any time in the year of assessment in which the relevant interest period ends, or in the previous tax year, will be excluded from this legislation, as will non-resident investors with no UK tax liabilities.

S1.4 Building society and bank deposit interest

The subject of interest *received* on building society accounts and bank deposits merits special emphasis, since evidence suggests that a surprisingly high proportion of depositors do not fully appreciate the way in which it is treated for tax purposes. In the first place, the rate of interest is expressed in 'net' or 'tax-paid' form, usually with the gross equivalent to a basic-rate taxpayer. Obviously, where the investor is liable to no more than basic-rate tax, this is straightforward enough, and there will be no further tax payable. However, the interest is assessable to higher rates of income tax where applicable (the Inland Revenue 'gross up' the depositor's declared net interest for this purpose), while, at the other end of the scale, the tax notionally paid at source cannot, in any circumstances, be reclaimed by investors whose tax liability does not extend to the basic rate, unlike other UK interest and dividend payments.

The conclusions to be drawn are as follows:

i Nil taxpayers should place their capital in investments where interest is paid gross or where tax deducted at source can be reclaimed – not in building society or bank deposit accounts.

ii Those investors liable to more than just the basic rate of tax should at least review any uncommitted deposits (i.e. those not earmarked for short-term expenditure, etc.) to see if better net returns are available elsewhere; for example, on low-coupon gilt-edged securities.

The foregoing considerations account for the apparently low rating of building society accounts as 'permanent' investments for the above categories of taxpayers in section 23.3. However it should be stressed that building society accounts can, in some circumstances, be recommended in preference to Stock Exchange securities (see, for example, section 2.1); in particular, they provide good capital liquidity and security, which means that they meet two major requirements of many private investors, especially those with limited capital resources.

The following table shows the true net yields at various tax rates on building society and bank deposit accounts, assuming (i) the interest is regarded as the last 'slice' of the depositor's income and (ii) the basic rate of tax is 29%.

Building society and bank deposit yields

'Net' rate paid	Equivalent gross yields		True net yields		
	Tax at:		Tax at:		
%	Nil %	29% and over %	Nil and 29% %	45% %	60% %
11.0	11.0	15.5	11.0	8.5	6.2
10.0	10.0	14.1	10.0	7.7	5.6
9.0	9.0	12.7	9.0	7.0	5.1
8.0	8.0	11.3	8.0	6.2	4.5
7.0	7.0	9.8	7.0	5.4	3.9
6.0	6.0	8.4	6.0	4.6	3.3
5.0	5.0	7.0	5.0	3.8	2.8

National Savings Bank accounts are excluded from these arrangements. This suggests that depositors with other institutions, who are not liable to tax on the interest earned, might consider switching their deposits to a National Savings Bank account or bond.

S1.5 Investment income strategy

The tax changes introduced progressively in Budgets since 1979 have considerably relieved the previously heavy burden of taxation borne by many investors. The highest possible marginal rate of tax is now 60%, following the abolition of the investment income surcharge on 6th April 1984. This means that many investors can obtain a higher income from their capital without, as often before, severely aggravating their tax liabilities. Nevertheless, there are some basic investment disciplines worth bearing in mind:

i   Try to make a realistic estimate of your true investment income requirements and arrange your capital accordingly. If, for example, you live comfortably within your earned income, review your investment position to see if any changes should be made to give a lower income but better capital growth potential, with the possibility of significant tax savings.

ii As a general rule, do not place large sums of money in deposit-type investments, such as those offered by building societies, banks and local authorities, on a long-term or indefinite basis if income is not a consideration, or if you are liable to higher rates of tax. Again, try to anticipate any major items of short-term expenditure, retain sufficient funds to cover these and at least take advice on reinvesting the rest.

iii Remember that capital gains are taxed at a maximum rate of 30% and, with careful planning, possibly much less (nil in certain cases – see following section on capital gains tax), which can be a significantly more attractive proposition for many investors, especially higher-rate taxpayers.

iv If your decision is to invest for a high income, bear in mind the eroding effects that inflation – rising prices – can have on a fixed level of income over the years. Rather than commit all your capital to fixed-interest securities, at least consider placing a proportion in equities – for example, income-orientated unit trusts – for their dividend growth potential, in any long-term investment programme, even if this means accepting a slightly lower initial income level.

Section S2
Capital gains tax

S2.1 Basis of charge 1986/87

Individuals

Where the total net gains of an individual, or husband and wife jointly, do not exceed £6,300 there will be no charge to CGT. All gains in excess of £6,300 will be taxed at a flat rate of 30%.

Losses incurred during the year will be set off against gains of the year, even if this reduces the net gains to less than £6,300. However, losses brought forward from a previous year will only be used to reduce the net gains to £6,300, any balance losses then remaining can again be carried forward.

Capital Gains Tax – individuals *(or husband and wife jointly)*
Tax payable on specimen gains

Assessable gain for year £	Tax payable £
Up to 6,300	Nil
7,000	210
10,000	1,110
15,000	2,610
20,000	4,110
30,000	7,110

Note: Even on gains of £20,000 in a single tax year the average tax rate is only 20.5% – considerably less than the 29% basic income tax rate.

Trustees

i *Settlements created before 7th June 1978.*
Where the total net gains of trusts do not exceed £3,150 there will be no charge to CGT. All gains in excess of £3,150 will be taxed at a flat rate of 30%. Losses incurred during the year will be set off against gains of the year, even if this reduces the net gains to less than £3,150. However, losses brought forward from a previous year will be used only to reduce the net gains to £3,150, any balance losses then remaining can again be carried forward.

ii *Settlements created on or after 7th June 1978*
The provisions will be similar to those for trusts created before 7th June 1978 (as above) except where the settler has created more than one such post-7th June 1978 trust. In that case the exempt slice will be the amount which results from dividing £3,150 by the number of such trusts, subject to a minimum exempt slice for each trust of £630.

Trustees of a settlement for a mentally disabled person or for a person in receipt of attendance allowance are assessed as individuals (see above), as are personal representatives of deceased persons in respect of gains accruing to the deceased's estate in the year of death and the two following years of assessment.

Future years

The exempt band will be increased in future years to reflect the change in RPI over the 12 months up to, and including, the December preceding the start of a new tax year; i.e. the exempt band is itself 'indexed', as well as the actual capital gain. For example, for 1987/88 the exempt band will be increased by an amount corresponding to the increase in the RPI between December 1985 and December 1986.

S2.2 Chargeable and exempt securities

The basis of charge referred to in section S2.1 relates to disposals of assets chargeable to capital gains tax. As far as stock market securities are concerned, these include ordinary shares and other classes of equity capital (including preference shares), fixed-interest stocks which are convertible into equity capital ('convertible stocks'), unit trusts, most offshore funds and foreign securities.

Certain securities, however, are exempt from capital gains tax altogether when they are sold or redeemed. These include all British Government stocks ('gilts') and local authority stocks and bonds. In addition, non-convertible UK industrial loan stocks and debentures are exempt, except where the holding arose from an original holding of a chargeable asset – for example, where a company issues fixed-interest loan stock wholly or partly in exchange for the ordinary shares of another company when acquiring or merging with that company.

S2.3 Pooling

The Finance Act 1985 reintroduced the concept of 'pooling', whereby multiple acquisitions of the same description, or 'class', are added together to create a single holding – the pool – for future capital gains tax purposes. However, it is possible for a holding of shares to comprise more than one pool for 'identification' purposes (see section S2.6) when a disposal occurs. The determining factor is the acquisition date. Subject to this, the following rules apply:

i   *Shares acquired before 6th April 1982*

Shares acquired before 6th April 1982 and still held at 5th April 1985 will constitute a separately identifiable pool. This pool, known as 'the 1982 holding', will be frozen until a disposal occurs. It cannot be increased by acquisitions after 5th April 1982 except, for example, by the 'allocation' of shares arising from a bonus or rights issue (see section S2.7).

Special rules apply to shares acquired before 6th April 1965, when capital gains tax was first introduced, and still held on 6th April 1985. Where the investor made an election under the Finance Act 1968 to substitute 6th April 1965 values for (earlier) purchase costs, the shares concerned will be included automatically in the 1982 holding (at their 6th April 1965 value) as described above.

Where such an election under the Finance Act 1968 was not made, pre-6th April 1965 acquisitions are treated as a separate pool. However, an election can be made so that they constitute (a) a new 1982 holding or (b) an addition to an existing 1982 holding if further acquisitions were made after 6th April 1965 and were still held on 6th April 1985. In both cases, the base cost will be their value at 6th April 1965.

In view of the potentially complex nature of the computations associated with pre-6th April 1965 shareholdings, it is recommended that investors seek professional guidance in order to ascertain their exact position with regard to capital gains tax.

ii   *Shares acquired between 6th April 1982 and 5th April 1985*
Shares acquired on or after 6th April 1982 and still held at 5th April 1985 will form a separate pool at 6th April 1985. This will be known as 'the new holding' to distinguish it from a 1982 holding as described in (i) above. This pool will increase or decrease by subsequent transactions in the shares.

iii   *Shares acquired wholly after 5th April 1985*
Shares acquired wholly after 5th April 1985, i.e. where a holding did not exist on that date, will be treated in a similar manner to that described under (ii) above except that, of course, the 6th April 1985 pool will not exist. Instead the pool will effectively commence in the month of the first acquisition of the shares.

S2.4 Indexation allowance

The indexation of gains for capital gains tax purposes was introduced in the 1982/83 tax year, i.e. with effect from 6th April 1982. Prior to that, chargeable gains or allowable losses were computed simply by taking the difference between the purchase cost of an asset and the proceeds when it was sold. This method, it was argued, was unfair to investors since it did not distinguish between real gains and 'illusory' gains arising from inflation.

This situation to some extent was remedied by the Finance Act 1982 which contained the Government's first attempt to counter inflation by introducing the concept of an indexation allowance. The rules have been modified in subsequent Finance Acts, the most recent changes appearing in the Finance Act 1985.

In theory, the purpose of the indexation allowance is simple enough; it removes inflation (at least, from March 1982 onwards) from the investment equation so that investors are taxed on real gains only. It is a notional item of allowable expenditure, determined by reference to movements in the Retail Prices Index (RPI), which is added to the actual cost of an investment for the purpose of calculating the chargeable gain or allowable loss when the investment is disposed of.

S2.5 Calculating the indexation allowance

In application, the new rules require the pool cost of a share-holding to be increased by the due indexation allowance each time a transaction (acquisition or disposal) occurs in the underlying shares. In practice, the actual calculation need not be made until a disposal occurs. The allowance is computed by applying to the cost the factor derived from the following formula:

$$\frac{RE - RL}{RL}$$

where RE = the RPI for the month of the new transaction (acquisition or disposal)

and RL = the RPI for the month when the previous transaction occurred or, if none has occurred since 5th April 1985, when the pool came into being (see below)

Special rules apply for the purpose of calculating the indexation allowance due on pools which existed at 6th April 1985. These can be summarised under the following headings:

  i *'1982 holdings'*

Pools comprising shares acquired before 6th April 1982 and forming a '1982 holding', as described in section S2.3 (i), will qualify for an indexation allowance based on the market value of the holding as at 31st March 1982, if the investor so elects. This will be to the investor's advantage if the market value at 31st March 1982 was greater than the pool cost, but, of course, it does require the 1982 holding to be revalued at 31st March 1982 to enable a comparison to be made.

Example

An investor made the following acquisition of PQR ordinary shares and still held the investment at 5th April 1985.

Date	No. shares	Cost
23.8.78	1,500	£1,000
17.1.80	2,500	£2,000

The price of PQR ordinary shares on 31st March 1982 was 200p.

The two acquisitions will be pooled to create a '1982 holding' of 4,000 PQR ordinary shares with a cost of £3,000. In August 1985 the investor sells all the shares for £12,000. The computations are as follows:

Pool cost	Value 31.3.82	Indexation factor	Indexation allowance	Indexed pool cost	Capital gain
£3,000	£8,000	0.2020*	£1,616	£4,616	£7,384

$$* \frac{376.7 \text{ (August 1985)} - 313.4 \text{ (March 1982)}}{313.4 \text{ (March 1982)}}$$

This example illustrates how, for '1982 holdings', the indexation allowance may be based on the 31st March 1982 value (although note that it is added to the pool cost for computing the capital gain or loss).

ii *6th April 1985 holdings*

Pools comprising shares acquired between 6th April 1982 and 5th April 1985 and forming a 'new holding', as described in section S2.3 (ii), will be increased by an indexation allowance calculated separately for each acquisition making up the pool by applying to the original cost(s) the following derivative of the above formula:

$$\frac{373.9 \text{ (the RPI for April 1985)} - RA}{RA}$$

where RA = the RPI for the month in which the relevant acquisition was made

This procedure will create an indexed pool cost (IPC) at 6th April 1985, so that the next indexation calculation, when a subsequent transaction occurs, will be based on the change in the RPI from April 1985 to the month of the new transaction.

Example 1

An investor made the following acquisitions of ordinary shares and still held the investments on 5th April 1985:

Date	(RPI)	Company	No. shares	Cost
17.2.83	327.3	ABC	2,000	£1,000
17.2.83	327.3	XYZ	2,000	£3,000
20.8.84	354.8	XYZ	1,000	£4,000

The indexed pool cost at 6th April 1985 will be calculated as follows:

Company	Shareholding 6.4.85	Cost	Indexation factor	Indexation allowance	Indexed pool cost
ABC	2,000	£1,000	.1423*	£142	£1,142
XYZ	(2,000)	(£3,000)	(.1423)*	(£427)	(£3,427)
	(1,000)	(£4,000)	(.0538)†	(£215)	(£4,215)
	3,000				£7,642

* $\dfrac{373.9 \text{ (April 1985)} - 327.3 \text{ (February 1983)}}{327.3 \text{ (February 1983)}}$

† $\dfrac{373.9 \text{ (April 1985)} - 354.8 \text{ (August 1984)}}{354.8 \text{ (August 1984)}}$

The pool holdings at 6th April 1985 are therefore 2,000 ABC ordinary shares and 3,000 XYZ ordinary shares with indexed pool costs of £1,142 and £7,642 respectively.

Example 2

Continuing the previous example, the investor acquired a further 2,000 XYZ ordinary shares on 20th August 1985 (RPI 376.7) at a cost of £5,000.

Before new transaction					*After new transaction*	
Holding	Indexed pool cost	Indexation factor	Indexation allowance	Updated IPC	Holding	Indexed pool cost
3,000	£7,642	.0075*	£57	£7,699	5,000	£12,699

* $\dfrac{376.7 \text{ (August 1985)} - 373.9 \text{ (April 1985)}}{373.9 \text{ (April 1985)}}$

This example illustrates the way in which a pool cost is increased by the due indexation allowance each time a transaction occurs.

In the event of a yet further acquisition of XYZ ordinary shares, the procedure would be repeated with the new indexed pool cost of £12,699 being increased by the relevant indexation allowance (between August 1985 and the month in which the further acquisition was made) before the further acquisition was added to the pool.

Example 3

Continuing the previous example again, the investor sold 2,000
XYZ ordinary shares for £8,000 in March 1987 (assume the RPI
is then 388.0 for illustration purposes). The computations are as
follows:

i   *Increase pool cost by the due indexation allowance*

Before new transaction

Holding	Indexed pool cost	Indexation factor	Indexation allowance	Increased IPC
5,000	£12,699	.0300*	£381	£13,080

ii   *Apportion cost†*

Shares sold $£13,080 \times \dfrac{2,000}{5,000} = £5,232$

Shares retained $£13,080 \times \dfrac{3,000}{5,000} = £7,848$

$$£13,080$$

Sale proceeds of 2,000 XYZ ordinary shares	£8,000
Apportioned cost	£5,232
Chargeable gain	£2,768

* $\dfrac{388.0 \text{ (assumed March 1987)} - 376.7 \text{ (August 1985)}}{376.7 \text{ (August 1985)}}$

† Since only part of the holding has been disposed of, the new indexed pool cost
must be apportioned on a pro rata basis between the part of the holding sold and
the part retained. The formula used to calculate the portion of the total cost
relevant to the shares sold is as follows:

Indexed pool cost $\times \dfrac{\text{No. of shares sold}}{\text{Total holding of shares}}$

The investor would thus retain 3,000 XYZ ordinary shares with
an updated indexed pool cost of £7,848.

It should be noted that a feature of the rules applicable to
disposals after 5th April 1985 is that the indexation allowance can
increase the size of a capital loss or create a loss in a no gain/no
loss situation (where sale proceeds are identical to purchase
cost). By the same token, an actual gain can be converted into an
allowable loss, i.e. where the indexation allowance is greater
than the actual gain. Therefore, if in example 3 above, the

investor had sold 2,000 XYZ ordinary shares for £3,000 (instead of £8,000 as shown) in March 1987, the allowable loss would be £2,232, i.e. apportioned cost of £5,232, less sale proceeds of £3,000.

S2.6 Identification

There is a defined process of 'identification' which must be adopted when a disposal is made. Identification in this context means the matching of the disposal with the appropriate holding or pool, as the case may be, where more than one acquisition occurred prior to the disposal.

Taking each disposal in chronological order, the sequence of identification will be as follows:

i   With acquisitions made on the same day as the disposal occurred, if any. Such transactions will not qualify for an indexation allowance.

ii With acquisitions made within a ten-day period before the disposal occurred, if any. Such transactions will not qualify for an indexation allowance.

iii With shares forming a post-1982 holding, or pool (as described in section S2.3 (ii) and (iii)), if any.

iv With shares forming a '1982 holding', or pool (as described in section S2.3 (i)), if any.

v   With shares forming a separate '1982 holding' derived from holdings which existed at 6th April 1965 in respect of which no original pooling election under the Finance Act 1968 has been made (as described also in section S2.3 (i)).

S2.7 Rights issues and capitalisation issues

Rights issues – shares taken up

Shares taken up via a rights issue are deemed to have been acquired at the same time as the original holding, although the cost is treated as a separate item of expenditure in the month in which it is incurred, i.e. the month in which the call is payable. Shares so received must be apportioned between any different 'pools' which might exist on a pro rata basis for identification purposes (see sections S2.3–S2.6).

Example

An investor made various acquisitions of ABC ordinary shares between January 1975 and January 1985 so that, at 5th April 1985, the following pools existed:

Pool	No. shares	Pool cost
'1982 holding'	4,000	£1,800
'New holding'	6,000	£5,200
(Totals)	(10,000)	(£7,000)

In August 1985, ABC makes a rights issue of 1 for 4 at 150p per share. The investor takes up his entitlement to 2,500 shares at a cost of £3,750. The rights must be allocated pro rata between the two pools. They will not be treated as simply an addition to the new holding (as would a normal purchase in the open market).

In this example, therefore, the 1982 holding would increase in August 1985 by 1,000 shares (and a cost of £1,500) and the new holding by 1,500 shares (and a cost of £2,250). However, the two existing pool costs of £1,800 and £5,200 would first be increased by the due indexation allowance in accordance with the procedures described in section S2.5.

Rights issues – sale of rights nil paid

Proceeds received from the sale of shares in nil paid form arising from a rights issue may be treated as a capital distribution, if small in relation to the market value of the underlying holding, and may be deducted from the original cost of the investment, i.e. excluded from the CGT computation for the year in which the sale was made. This lower cost figure will then be used as the basis for assessing any future CGT liability on the remaining holding. The Inland Revenue will normally regard amounts not exceeding 5% of the market value of the holding as small. A similar ruling applies to other small capital distributions.

Where the amount exceeds 5% of the market value of the holding, it will be treated as a disposal, and the cost must be apportioned between the 'old' holding and the 'cash' proceeds by reference to the market value of the 'old' shares at the date of disposal of the rights in nil paid form. The calculations necessary to establish the indexation allowance due on such a disposal and to adjust the pool cost(s) can involve protracted arithmetical effort and investors in doubt as to their potential liability on such a disposal should consult a qualified tax adviser.

Capitalisation issues

Capitalisation issues, in effect, are treated as rights issues with a nil cost in that they must be apportioned between any different 'pools' which might exist for identification purposes.

Example

Refer to the previous example. Assume that instead of a rights issue in August 1985, ABC makes a capitalisation issue of 1 for 4. The 2,500 shares received by the investor would be allocated on the same basis between the two pools, which would retain their original costs of £1,800 and £5,200 respectively.

S2.8 'Bed and breakfast' transactions

'Bed and breakfast' was the popular name given to a stock market dealing procedure whereby an investor could sell a holding of shares just prior to the close of business one day and repurchase them, at only a marginally higher cost, immediately the market reopened the next day. This practice was widely used by investors as a CGT manoeuvre and, depending upon the circumstances, enabled capital gains or losses to be established whilst effectively retaining the shares (other than overnight).

The complex rules of 'identification' which accompanied the introduction of indexation (in operation from 6th April 1982) effectively rendered obsolete this practice, although the same result could still be achieved by spreading the sale and repurchase over two Stock Exchange accounting periods. This, however, was potentially a more costly exercise.

A strict interpretation of the rules effective from 6th April 1985 suggests that 'bed and breakfast' transactions as originally understood are again permissible. However, the two sides of the transaction need to be at 'arms length', i.e. not prearranged, in order to be accepted by the Inland Revenue as an unrelated sale and repurchase. It is recommended that investors contemplating such transactions should first consult their usual adviser.

A point to remember is that a 'bed and breakfast' transaction involving only part of a holding may have implications for future transactions in the shares. For example, where a shareholding was acquired wholly before 6th April 1982 (and thereby forms a 1982 holding as described in section S2.3 (i)) a partial sale followed by a repurchase of those shares would create a separate pool, i.e. a new holding as described in section S2.3 (ii). Thus, any subsequent partial disposals would be identified first with the latter pool, in accordance with the rules set out in section S2.6. Generally speaking and where circumstances permit, it is, therefore, preferable to 'bed and breakfast' an entire holding of shares so that a single new pool is created for future CGT purposes.

S2.9 Capital gains tax strategy

That no one wants to pay more tax than is taken 'unavoidably' from their income is an entirely understandable sentiment and, of course, CGT in particular can be avoided simply by not making a disposal of the assets concerned (unless there is no alternative) or, at least, by keeping the net gain within the annual exemption (see section S2.1). It is certainly true that the widening of the exempt band in recent years has given investors much more flexibility to change their portfolios while avoiding CGT, yet many now seem to regard the exemption as a ceiling which must not be exceeded, regardless of the underlying case for doing so, i.e. where analysis of the future prospects for the shareholding concerned suggests there is a good reason for selling it at the prevailing price, even though such action may result in a CGT liability. The reverse is often true also, in that many investors show a marked reluctance to sell investments at a loss. If such a situation can be ascribed solely to the general market trend, then by all means hold the investment for recovery when sentiment improves. However, if the outlook for the shareholding has deteriorated it is often more sensible to grasp the nettle, accept the loss and look for better potential elsewhere.

So, as the end of the tax year approaches, investors should be looking at their portfolios and any transactions already carried out with the following points in mind:

i   Do not let CGT considerations alone override any sound fundamental reasons for changing investments. The paramount question should always be: is the investment worth holding at its prevailing market price?

ii   Consider very carefully the benefits, i.e. potential tax advantages, of selling and immediately repurchasing shareholdings simply to establish a gain or loss – these may be minimal (see section S2.8).

iii Generally speaking, it is preferable, where possible, to absorb any unused portion of the annual exemption by portfolio adjustments such as (a) 'top-slicing' overweight holdings in order to diversify, (b) upgrading the quality of an investment with perhaps questionable potential or (c), at the other end of the scale, consolidating those small or fragmented holdings which tend to accumulate in private investment portfolios.

iv   If realised gains exceed the exempt slice (see section S2.1) and no losses are being carried forward from the previous year, examine the cost position of any other holdings in case there are allowable losses available which could be established to reduce the gain to the exempt figure. Remember, however, that current year losses will be set against current year gains, even if this reduces the net gain to less than the exempt figure.

v   Remember that events such as (a) the redemption of certain negotiable fixed-interest securities, (b) the receipt of cash from takeovers or mergers and (c) the sale of rights issues, capital distributions, etc. (but see section S2.7), all may count as disposals for capital gains tax purposes, as may the transfer of securities or other chargeable assets to children or other persons, except between husband and wife.

Section S3
Personal Equity Plan Scheme

S3.1 What is a Personal Equity Plan?

The Personal Equity Plan ('PEP') was first introduced in the March 1986 Budget but comes into effect on 1st January 1987. Its purpose is to encourage more investment by individuals in UK companies, especially new or smaller investors. Plan holders must be over 18 years of age and resident in the United Kingdom for tax purposes.

A PEP will offer tax relief to investors who invest up to £2,400 a year in UK equities, but the underlying PEP must be administered by an approved PEP manager, who will be responsible, inter alia, for all necessary reporting to the Inland Revenue. At no time will the investor need to advise the Inland Revenue of the fact that he or she has taken out a PEP, or of the investment transactions and dividends arising within the plan. Simplicity for the investor has thus been given high priority in the design of PEPs.

There will be two basic types of PEPs available, namely non-discretionary PEPs and discretionary PEPs. The first of these will leave the initial choice of investments and the subsequent management of the PEP portfolio to the investor, the PEP manager being used by the investor to execute his or her instructions and to fulfil the required administrative functions.

The discretionary scheme will normally involve common management of a limited choice of portfolios with different objectives, e.g. income, growth or a balance between the two, for investors who choose this option. The PEP manager will have full discretion over the composition and management of the portfolios but within them will allocate specific shareholdings to individual PEPs to comply with the requirement that the investor is a direct shareholder in the underlying companies.

The maximum annual contribution of £2,400 may be invested as a lump sum or as regular (not less than monthly) payments. Although, in practice, the relatively high dealing costs that the latter would incur means that investors who do adopt this course will almost certainly be best advised to elect for a discretionary scheme as described above.

Investments allocated to a PEP must be made in cash. What this means, in effect, is that an investor's existing shareholdings cannot be transferred to a PEP. Qualifying investments are the ordinary shares of UK companies with a full Stock Exchange listing, i.e. excluding, for example, shares of companies quoted on the Unlisted Securities Market. However, up to £420, or 25% of the annual subscription, whichever is the higher, may be invested in authorised unit trusts or recognised investment trusts (the latter otherwise being excluded as qualifying investments). Uninvested cash can be held within a plan, subject to certain limits.

Contributions to a particular PEP must be made in a single calendar year and the plan kept open for at least the whole of the following calendar year. This qualifying period could thus vary in length from 12 months 1 day (for plans taken out on 31st December) to up to 24 months (for plans taken out in early January). Within this period, all investments and income must be retained within the plan. In other words, the investor will not receive any direct income from the underlying investments, but it will be used to build up the capital value.

Withdrawals of shares or cash from a plan invalidates it with effect from the initial contribution date. Investors wishing to invest in a PEP in consecutive years will have to arrange a new PEP each year, i.e. additional investments cannot be made in a previous year's plan.

A factor crucial to the concept of the scheme is that the investor is the beneficial owner of the underlying shares so that he may participate as much as any other shareholder. So, although typically the shares will be registered in the name of the PEP manager's nominee company and the actual share certificates held by the plan manager, the latter is obliged to ensure that the investor receives the annual report and accounts of the companies in which he or she holds shares and, if the investor so wishes, arrange for him or her to attend shareholder's meetings, exercise voting rights and receive other shareholder information.

PEP managers themselves must be authorised securities dealers and in due course will need to be authorised investment businesses under the Financial Services Bill (see section 1.3). The details of the plans that various large organisations, such as the clearing banks, will be offering are beginning to emerge as this guide goes to print. These indicate that most will be offering a limited 'menu' of perhaps 30 to 50 leading shares which investors can choose from on a non-discretionary basis, with investments in shares outside of this list probably attracting an additional charge. Discretionary plans will also in practice be generally geared to the shares of large companies.

S3.2 The tax benefits

Section S3.1 described in broad detail what will constitute a PEP. Clearly, the scheme has fairly tightly defined rules, but what is the benefit to the investor?

The attraction of a PEP is that once it has existed for the qualifying period of between one and two years, all reinvested dividends and interest and all capital gains will be entirely free of tax while, as mentioned in section S3.1, the investor is relieved of all contact with the Inland Revenue, at least as far as the PEP is concerned. On the face of it, this sounds an attractive proposition and for the investor prepared to take a long-term view a PEP will be well worth considering.

However, there are two points to bear in mind. First, under current capital gains tax legislation invididuals are in any event permitted to realise capital gains of £6,300 in a single tax year (see section S2.1), which means that the capital gains tax 'benefit' of a PEP is unlikely to prove particularly worthwhile for a small investor, at least for many years. Secondly, the income tax saving on dividends generated by shareholdings in a PEP is not going to amount to very much, particularly in the first few years. For example, a £2,400 investment in shares yielding 5% would in a full year produce £120 gross income, on which the tax saving would be around £35 to a basic rate taxpayer.

Against this must be weighed the cost of taking out the plan. From a PEP manager's point of view, plans are going to be quite expensive to administer which is likely to make a PEP a more highly-priced method of investing than ordinary share dealing procedures.

On balance, a PEP is probably worth considering by the new or smaller investor prepared to take a long-term view, particularly those seeking to invest with minimum fuss on a regular basis. However, the type of investor to whom PEPs look most appealing is the investor who already has a portfolio of investments showing large capital gains and who can therefore benefit more directly by building up tax-free funds through a PEP.

Section S4

Inheritance tax

The March 1986 Budget included proposals to reform the taxation of capital movements between individuals by (i) abolishing capital transfer tax on lifetime transfers and (ii) renaming the tax 'inheritance tax'. This book can offer no general advice on the subject but, for information purposes, the rate of charge is given below.

S4.1 Scale of charge

Effective 19th March 1986

Bands of chargeable value	On death*
Amount £	Rate %
0 – 71,000	Nil
71,001 – 95,000	30
95,001 – 129,000	35
129,001 – 164,000	40
164,001 – 206,000	45
206,001 – 257,000	50
257,001 – 317,000	55
Over 317,000	60

*Transfers made within seven years before death will be charged on a tapered scale.

The Stock Exchange

Regional offices and addresses

A list of Stock Exchange publications or member firms willing to accept approaches from new clients can be obtained from the offices of The Stock Exchange listed below.

Information and Press Department,
The Stock Exchange,
London EC2N 1HP

or The Stock Exchange at:
10 High Street, Belfast BT1 2BP.
Margaret Street, Birmingham B3 3JL.
28 Anglesea Street, Dublin 2.
69 St George's Place, Glasgow G2 1BU.
4 Norfolk Street, Manchester M2 1BS.
Melrose House, 3 St Sampson's Square, York YO1 2RL.

Visitors' gallery of the London Stock Exchange

The Stock Exchange visitors' gallery, overlooking the trading floor, is open to the public on normal business days from 9.45 a.m. to 3.15 p.m. Brief commentaries by the Guides in attendance are given throughout the day, while a 20 minute film about The Stock Exchange is also shown at regular intervals. The gallery is well worth a visit, but parties wishing to see the film are advised to book in advance.

Index